FRENCH FILM DIRECTORS

Bertrand Blier

SUE HARRIS

Manchester University Press
MANCHESTER AND NEW YORK

distributed exclusively in the USA by Palgrave

The right of Sue Harris to be identified as the author of this work has been asserted by her in accordance with the Copyright, Designs and Patents Act 1988.

Published by Manchester University Press
Oxford Road, Manchester M13 9NR, UK
and Room 400, 175 Fifth Avenue, New York, NY 10010, USA
http://www.manchesteruniversitypress.co.uk

Distributed exclusively in the USA by
Palgrave, 175 Fifth Avenue, New York,
NY 10010, USA

Distributed exclusively in Canada by
UBC Press, University of British Columbia, 2029 West Mall,
Vancouver, BC, Canada V6T 1Z2

British Library Cataloguing-in-Publication Data
A catalogue record for this book is available from the British Library

Library of Congress Cataloging-in-Publication Data applied for

ISBN 0 7190 5296 3 *hardback*
     0 7190 5297 1 *paperback*

First published 2001

10 09 08 07 06 05 04 03 02 01   10 9 8 7 6 5 4 3 2 1

Typeset in Scala with Meta display
by Koinonia, Manchester
Printed in Great Britain
by Bookcraft (Bath) Ltd, Midsomer Norton

Bertrand Blier

MANCHESTER
UNIVERSITY PRESS

FRENCH FILM DIRECTORS

DIANA HOLMES and ROBERT INGRAM *series editors*
DUDLEY ANDREW *series consultant*

Luc Besson SUSAN HAYWARD

Robert Bresson KEITH READER

Claude Chabrol GUY AUSTIN

Diane Kurys CARRIE TARR

Georges Méliès ELIZABETH EZRA

Jean Renoir MARTIN O'SHAUGHNESSY

Coline Serreau BRIGITTE ROLLET

François Truffaut DIANA HOLMES AND ROBERT INGRAM

Agnès Varda ALISON SMITH

Contents

List of plates

Figures 1–3 are reproduced by permission of CAPAC (Compagnie artistique de productions et d'adaptations cinématiques). Figures 8 and 9 are reproduced by permission of Hachette Première. Figures 4–6, 8 and 10 are reproduced courtesy of BFI Films: Stills, Posters and Designs. Every effort has been made to obtain permission to reproduce the figures illustrated in this book. If any proper acknowledgement has not been made, copyright-holders are invited to contact the publisher.

Series editors' foreword

To an anglophone audience, the combination of the words 'French' and 'cinema' evokes a particular kind of film: elegant and wordy, sexy but serious – an image as dependent on national stereotypes as is that of the crudely commercial Hollywood blockbuster, which is not to say that either image is without foundation. Over the past two decades, this generalised sense of a significant relationship between French identity and film has been explored in scholarly books and articles, and has entered the curriculum at university level and, in Britain, at A-level. The study of film as an art-form and (to a lesser extent) as industry, has become a popular and widespread element of French Studies, and French cinema has acquired an important place within Film Studies. Meanwhile, the growth in multi-screen and 'art-house' cinemas, together with the development of the video industry, has led to the greater availability of foreign-language films to an English-speaking audience. Responding to these developments, this series is designed for students and teachers seeking information and accessible but rigorous critical study of French cinema, and for the enthusiastic filmgoer who wants to know more.

The adoption of a director-based approach raises questions about *auteurism*. A series that categorises films not according to period or to genre (for example), but to the person who directed them, runs the risk of espousing a romantic view of film as the product of solitary inspiration. On this model, the critic's role might seem to be that of discovering continuities, revealing a necessarily coherent set of themes and motifs which correspond to the particular genius of the individual. This is not our aim: the *auteur* perspective on film, itself most clearly articulated in France in the early 1950s, will be interrogated in certain volumes of the series, and, throughout, the director will be treated as one highly significant element in a complex process of film production and reception which includes socio-economic and political determinants, the work of a large and highly skilled team of artists and technicians, the mechanisms of production and distribution, and the complex and multiply determined responses of spectators.

The work of some of the directors in the series is already known outside France, that of others is less so – the aim is both to provide informative and original English-language studies of established figures, and to extend the range of French directors known to anglophone students of cinema. We intend the series to contribute to the promotion of the informal and formal study of French films, and to the pleasure of those who watch them.

DIANA HOLMES
ROBERT INGRAM

Acknowledgements

I wish to express my sincere thanks to the many friends, colleagues and family members who have offered encouragement, support and practical help during the writing of this book. I acknowledge, in particular, a huge debt of gratitude to Jill Forbes, Siân Reynolds, Keith Reader and Elizabeth Ezra, whose erudition and enthusiasm for my work have been utterly invaluable. Pauline Fower, Louise Stirton, Kathy Magarrell, Louise Douglas and Audrey Farley have all offered support well beyond the call of duty, as have the friends in Amiens and Paris who have provided accommodation and a warm welcome during my various research trips to France. I have greatly appreciated the suggestions and advice offered by Diana Holmes and Robert Ingram, who have been patient and supportive editors. I extend my thanks also to Radio France Culture, for providing me with a recording of the broadcast 'Le bon plaisir de Bertrand Blier', and to the staff of Stirling University Library, the Bibliothèque de l'Arsenal and the Bibliothèque du Film in Paris. And, like all who teach film studies, I am indebted to my students who have shared their reactions to Blier's films with me, with good humour and insight.

My final thanks are reserved for my husband Neil Harris, who has lived with Bertrand Blier and his films as long as I have, and who has been a constant source of practical and emotional support. In recognition of this, it is to him and our son Euan that I dedicate this book, with love and thanks.

Introduction

The director Bertrand Blier has, over a thirty-year period, come to be acknowledged as one of the most enduring and challenging talents of French post-new wave cinema. In that time, he has enjoyed a fruitful, if volatile, relationship with both critics and the viewing public, being variously fêted and derided, applauded and jeered for his provocative approach to modern film-making. His commercial success, although inconsistent, has been impressive and he has been at many points in his career the object of significant peer recognition: an Academy Award for Best Foreign Film (*Préparez vos mouchoirs*) and a clutch of *Césars* attest to this. In addition to directing fourteen films of his own, he has ventured at various points in his career into the writing of screenplays, novels and, most recently, a play, showing himself to be an ambitious, creative and highly successful artist in a range of media. His influence on a younger generation of film-makers in the French industry has been equally remarkable: Patrice Leconte, Michel Blanc and Josiane Balasko are only the most prominent of those whose thematic and stylistic priorities reflect and emulate Blier's own.

It is, as we shall see, the very unconventionality of this work that has had such an appeal to emerging film-makers and actors. But this unconventionality has also proved confusing for many viewers: critics have, since the earliest films, documented the extent to which Blier's work has left cinema-goers amused, perplexed and offended, not always in equal measure. Some have taken the view, for example, that his exuberant portrayal of sexual activity is suggestive of an ultra-libertarian sensibility, but many have read the more anarchistic elements of his work as profoundly reactionary. Some consider the man to be a playful puppet-master inverting the conventions and genres of gender representation, but for others he has been deemed a dangerous subversive who would do well to keep his macho fantasies under wraps. Viewers and critics have long failed to reach consensus on whether we should laugh or be horrified at the dysfunctional characters and societies set out before us, about whether we can interpret his films as comic explorations of the grotesque, or as misanthropic attacks on the frailties of human nature.

Ultimately, there is some validity in categorising Blier as one of the most difficult, irritating and incomprehensible of contemporary French film-makers, one whose work is to be approached with caution, and is to be analysed in terms of the exception, rather than the rule of mainstream French cinema. And yet the notoriety that has grown up around him and his corpus of fourteen films has in many ways served only to obscure our vision of what is clearly an intelligent and reflective *auteur*, working within the traditions of intellectual and theoretical engagement common to the wider French cinema industry. Whether one 'likes' his work or not, Blier is undisputably an important and influential presence in modern French film-making, and for those who would understand the nature and function of popular French culture, it has now become impossible to ignore his work. He may well be a maverick figure, but his abiding presence and obvious creativity inevitably speak for themselves, and point to the director as a figure worthy of the same critical attention as canonical luminaries such as Truffaut, Renoir, Chabrol and the other directors on which this series seeks to focus.

The intention of this book is therefore simple: in attempting to address some of the questions put above, I hope to be able to start formulating some answers to the puzzle that is Bertand Blier's work. The aim is not to make the case for Blier as a misunderstood exponent of mainstream cinema and insist that that is where he really belongs, but rather to identify strategies for finding one's way through a body of work which has disconcerted spectators, critics and academics alike, and to identify some reference points which the curious spectator can use as a map to navigate through Blier's preferred themes and stylistic techniques. By reappraising some of the received wisdom about the director's work, and identifying a counter-cultural context in which his work might profitably be read, it should be possible to evaluate Blier's contribution to modern French film-making more fully than has hitherto been the case. The analysis in this book therefore goes directly to the heart of the perceived difficulty with Blier's work, confronting questions about corporeality in the *mise-en-scène*, scatological content in dialogue and aggressivity in the portrayal of social interaction, in an attempt to locate Blier's work in culturally marginalised traditions which have their own aesthetic and historical value.

The discussion will reveal that the key tropes around which Blier's work is structured point to an engagement with a tradition of popular discourse, here translated into both content and form, which finds an echo in the wider cultural apparatus of the post-1968 period, and which is all the more significant for its location in mainstream visual culture. The concept of artistic subversion is absolutely central to understanding Blier's work: subversion in the popular tradition is about more than simply offending notions of good taste and behaviour, but is instead about an active engagement with patterns of disruption and parody, a valorising of the profane over the purely antagonistic. Popular culture has been greatly served by the analysis of traditional forms offered by Mikhail Bakhtin in his seminal work *Rabelais and his World*, which allowed for a re-evaluation of an enigmatic body of work, by a writer of whom Bakhtin says on his opening page '[O]f all great writers of world literature, [he] is the least popular, the least understood and appreciated. And yet, of all the great creators of European literature Rabelais occupies one of the first places' (Bakhtin 1984: 1).

Sixteenth-century literature may seem an unusual place to start an analysis of the work of a contemporary French film director, but the parallels that we can detect between the aesthetic choices and resulting discourses of the two artists are helpful when seeking to categorise the content and structure of their work. As Sue Vice points out: 'Bahktin reveals that Rabelais has been misunderstood, his grotesque images misread as simple political allegories or as obscenity and "cynicism"; replacing him in the tradition of popular humour gives a quite different dimension to his aesthetic' (Vice 1997: 191). And so it is with Bertrand Blier. When one attempts to move beyond the 'meaning' of Blier's work, and assessments of him as a 'failed realist' or amoral *agent provocateur*, and looks instead at the formal construction of his work – its rhetorical structure, complex verbal layering, ritualistic composition – then a clear cultural context in which Blier's work 'makes sense' quickly emerges. Bakhtin's concept of carnival is a useful place to start in as much as it invites a reading of Blier's humour as festive and ludic rather than wilfully aggressive, his characters as stock types rather than hideous incarnations of urban menace, his language as a celebration of linguistic diversity rather than a bald expression of offensive vulgarity.

The concept of *la fête* (the festive) which Bakhtin elaborated has a wider significance in Blier's work than the purely formal. Bakhtin's work, first published in 1970, was only one of a number of important texts which developed an understanding of cultural debate and production in post-1968 France in terms of the traditional carnival's associations with concepts of festivity, revolution, liberation of energies and subversion of discourses of authority.[1] As Brian Rigby has made clear, *la fête* has become a talismanic word in French cultural discourse, gaining in currency in the postwar period, and especially since 1968, and it has now become relatively commonplace to refer to the events of 1968 – an acknowledged moment of social and cultural transition in which privilege, social rank and prohibition were systematically questioned – using the rhetorical framework of carnivalesque or festive analysis (Rigby 1991). Contemporary ethnographers and cultural commentators also began to analyse cultural practices and events in

---

[1] The 1970s saw the publication of two important historical texts on this subject, the first by Mona Ozouf, *La Fête révolutionnaire* (1976), and the second *Le Carnaval de Romans* (1979) by Emmanuel Le Roy Ladurie.

relation to *culture ordinaire* (everyday culture), and the revolutionary potential of the *fête* was reformulated by writers such as Henri
Lefèbvre, who identified the possibility for cultural revolution as
lying within marginalised groups in society such as the young,
ethnic minorities and women.

The performance arts also experienced a renewed interest in
the dramatic forms of popular spectacle; indeed, the tone, content
and type of performance of Total Theatre, *création collective* (experimental collective theatre such as that performed by the *Théâtre du
soleil*) and *café-théâtre* expressed the festivity and aesthetic subversion of an art-form emerging directly from, and addressing *le
peuple* (the people). The Situationists equally elaborated an ideology
of *détournement* (a strategy of appropriation of bourgeois concepts
of representation with the aim of subverting them) which gave
momentum to the cultural mood of the times. In cinema, Jacques
Doillon's *L'An 01* (1972) is representative of a new style of film
which, as Jill Forbes has pointed out, shows 'youthful exuberance,
transgression and anarchy ... It consists of a series of sketches or
situations designed to illustrate, praise or promote the transgression of bureaucratic rules and the liberation from all forms of
oppression' (Forbes 1992: 201–2). Even journalism was not
exempt from this particular cultural trend, as a ludic, and at times
exceedingly juvenile, commentary found expression in the new
subversive magazine culture represented by *Hara-Kiri*, *Charlie
Hebdo*, *Pilote* and the enormous popularity of the *bande dessinée*
(cartoon strip). This generalised new interest in modes of expression deriving directly from popular festive forms, drew with great
frequency on the central motif of the carnival, which came
increasingly to be reflected, in cinema as elsewhere in popular
culture, in the adoption of anarchic narrative structures, an
iconography of youth, and in an explicit discourse of challenge to
social, political and artistic hierarchies. The apparatus of Bakhtinian discourse analysis, understood in terms of an association
with generalised cultural trends in modern French society, is thus
a key tool in working towards a considered understanding of the
aesthetic, humour and cultural contexts of Bertrand Blier's films.

References

Bakhtin, Mikhail (1984), *Rabelais and his World* (trans. Hélène Iswolsky), Bloomington, Indiana University Press.

Forbes, Jill (1992), *The Cinema in France: After the New Wave*, London, Macmillan.

Ozouf, Mona (1976), *La Fête révolutionnaire*, Paris, Gallimard.

Lefèbvre, Henri (1968), *La Vie quotidienne dans le monde moderne*, Paris, Gallimard.

Le Roy Ladurie, Emmanuel (1979), *Le Carnaval de Romans*, Paris, Gallimard.

Rigby, Brian (1991), *Popular Culture in Modern France: a Study of Cultural Discourse*, London and New York, Routledge.

Vice, Sue (1997), *Introducing Bakhtin*, Manchester, Manchester University Press.

1

'L'impossible Monsieur B. B ...'[1]

Bertrand Blier was born in Paris on 14 March 1939. As was still relatively conventional in the French film-making tradition, his career began in 1957 as an *assistant stagiaire* (trainee assistant). Promoted by Serge Vallin, a friend of his actor father Bernard Blier (a well-known and well-loved character actor with a long and distinguished career in France) and assistant to leading directors such as Renoir, Becker and Duvivier, Blier's first involvement in film-making was as an assistant on the John Berry film *OK Mambo* (1959). In 1958 and 1959, Blier worked with the same status on films directed by Christian-Jaque (*Babette s'en va-t-en guerre*, 1959), Delannoy (*Maigret et l'affaire Saint-Fiacre*, 1959) and La Patellière (*Rue des prairies*, 1959), before graduating in 1960 to the status of second assistant with the director Georges Lautner. With Lautner, Blier worked for over two years (1960–61) on four moderately successful films (*Arrêtez les tambours*, 1960; *Le Monocle noir*, 1961; *Le Septième juré*, 1961; *En plein cirage*, 1961) all very much in the 'veine parodique' ('parodic style', (Jeancolas 1979: 149)) that has come to characterise his own work.

The story so far does not disguise the fact that Blier's initial career benefited from some considerable advantages and privileges.[2] He

1 'The impossible Mr B. B ...' (Riou 1993: 58).
2 Blier is described by Jeancolas (1979: 137) as a 'dauphin de divers pouvoirs' ('the heir apparent of various powers'), as opposed to someone who came into the industry via a more conventional route. The convention, broken by the *Cahiers du cinéma* critics and directors, was to serve a virtual apprenticeship at the level of assistant for a long number of years.

was lucky enough to profit from being born into an exceptionally artistic family of some renown, and it is certain that his father's contact with a circle of prestigious celebrity friends set Blier, very early in his life, at the centre of a creative and intellectual environment, which would inevitably prove influential in his work and style. Other prominent family members include a paternal grandfather who was a member of La Société des amis de Charles Dullin, one of the 1930s theatrical Cartel des Quatre, and a mother who abandoned a career as a professional musician to raise a family and support her husband's acting career. His godfather was the great French actor Louis Jouvet (another of the Cartel), although it appears that Blier remained ignorant of this fact until adulthood, and other family friends included the film director Henri-Georges Clouzot, the playwright Marcel Achard, and the actor François Périer, the man acknowledged by the mature Blier as 'mon deuxième père' ('my second father' (France Culture 1995)).

Given Blier's privileged contact with individuals from the French theatre and cinema worlds, his professional movement towards the milieu was perhaps unsurprising, and his background clearly allowed him possibilities that were perhaps denied other young film-makers of his age, an advantage that he has never sought to deny.[3] And yet his relative failure to establish himself firmly in the profession over the first fourteen years of his career bears out his defence that 'la réputation d'un père ne peut pas tout dans une profession où le moindre film réclame des millions d'investissement' (Riou: 59)[4] confirming that Blier's eventual success as a major film-maker has been above all a consequence of his own talent and endeavour.

3 'C'est évidemment très agréable d'être le fils d'un acteur connu ... Mais mon père m'a apporté bien davantage qu'un petit prestige scolaire immédiat ... Le fait d'être élevé dans une maison où venaient constamment des gens drôles constitue une chance énorme.' ('Of course it's great to be the son of a famous actor ... but my father gave me much more than a bit of prestige at school. Being brought up in a house always full of amusing people was a wonderful piece of good fortune' (Riou 1993: 58–9)).
4 'A father's reputation isn't everything in an industry where even the most basic film needs millions of francs of investment.'

Blier's definitive break with *l'assistanat* came in 1962, when he was offered a directing role on a *cinéma-vérité* project being produced by André Michelin of the famous industrial Michelin family. This first feature-length film, *Hitler, connais pas!*, was released in Paris on 25 July 1963, when Blier was 24 years old, and like many of the films to follow, this film was the subject of considerable controversy. Deselected from the main Cannes Film Festival in May 1963 on the grounds that it was 'trop intellectuel' ('too intellectual' (Haustrate 1988: 13)), not an accusation which has continued to be levelled at Blier's work, the film went on to be presented 'hors sélection' and was favourably reviewed by festival critics. *Hitler, connais pas!* is an important film which shows Blier working within a studio-bound and non-realist cinematic tradition, and thereby taking an alternative creative approach to that of his groundbreaking contemporaries in the *nouvelle vague* movement. Furthermore, *Hitler, connais pas!* is a film which signalled from the outset Blier's focus on a dramatic style of cinema. He himself acknowledges it as an important film, a 'film nourricier' ('source film' (France Culture 1995)) which continues to inform his approaches to characterisation, theme and narrative form in his mature work, and the film can therefore be read as an important vehicle of experimentation for the director's later film projects.

This début film first created the kind of stir that has come to characterise all Blier's subsequent releases. Yet the relatively common assessment of this film in terms of 'un déshabillage moral inquiétant et malsain' ('a worrying and unhealthy process of revelation' (Hauttecœur 1963: 5)) sat oddly with more favourable evaluations which unambiguously acknowledged the talent at work in the film, and announced Blier as an important and cinematically astute new director. Daringly, one critic expressed this view in the following terms: 'Le film de Bertrand Blier constitue une très grande réussite dans la recherche d'une expression nouvelle cinématographique. Que signifieront dans cinquante ou cent ans, pour les historiens du cinéma, les fameuses initiales 'BB'? Brigitte Bardot ... ou Bertrand Blier?' ('Blier's film is an exciting achievement in the quest for new cinematic expressions. What will the famous initials 'B.B.' mean to cinema historians fifty or a hundred years from now? Brigitte Bardot ... or Bertrand Blier?' (Jeander 1963: 5)).

This tentative, but nonetheless auspicious beginning was followed by a period of great activity, but little actual success. Blier spent this time writing screenplays and adaptations which ultimately came to nothing, but which were highly personal pieces, before going on to make a short film, *La Grimace* (1966). However, the only feature-length film that he managed to bring to completion, *Même si j'étais un espion* (1967), a topical if unremarkable contribution to the then filmic vogue for spy thrillers, starring Bruno Cremer and his father, was received, by both critics and public alike, with little real enthusiasm.[5] A commercial flop for Blier, the film has been little commented on in subsequent analyses of his work, and yet it has some importance in the Blier canon, establishing through a narrative exploration of fear and isolation the absurd qualities and key themes that Blier would build upon in his mature film-making, particularly in *Buffet froid* (1979) and *Notre histoire* (1984). However, in terms of Blier's overall work, this is seen as a forgotten film, one that is no longer in distribution, and given that Blier was only one of a team of five scriptwriters on the project, and had arguably at this stage in his career not yet worked out what would be the stamp of his own work, it is ultimately a less profitable vehicle than the subsequent works for exploring Blier's own auteurist conception.

An opportunity was provided once again by Georges Lautner, who commissioned him to write the screenplay of his film *Laisse aller... c'est une valse* (1970), described by Lautner as 'un vaudeville policier traité comme une bande dessinée' ('a vaudevillesque thriller, in comic-strip style' (Tulard 1995: 9)), and the film was moderately successful in France at the time of its release. Blier's frustration at not being able to establish a directorial career in

5 This film reflected thematically the contemporary mood at the end of the cold war, and the film's release coincided with the vogue in France for the spy-thriller novels of John Le Carré. Blier's view is that 'J'avais la prétention, à l'époque, de proposer une réflexion sur le fascisme. Mais je manquais de la maturité nécessaire pour la maîtriser' ('I was pretentious enough to think that I was making a film about Fascism. But I wasn't sufficiently mature to bring it off' (Haustrate 1988: 19)).

film-making, together with his relative success as a screenwriter for others prompted him to explore other forms of writing, and by the early 1970s Blier had to all intents and purposes abandoned cinema and turned his attention to novel writing. Ironically, the publication of the novel *Les Valseuses* in 1971 was to prove to be the major turning point in Blier's cinematic career. Almost immediately, he was approached with propositions to adapt it for the screen, which he did in 1973 to considerable acclaim: the film was a huge box-office hit, and was second in the year's ratings only to the first of the blockbuster soft-porn series *Emmanuelle* (Jaekin, 1973).

Les Valseuses was then, an enormous *succès de scandale*, and many critics adopted a suitably scandalised tone in their discussion of it. One critic declared that 'le plus triste, c'est que le talent de Blier et de ses comédiens soit mis au service d'une telle entreprise' ('the saddest thing is that the talent of Blier and his actors should have been wasted on such a venture' (Tremois 1974: 63)), another that this was 'un film authentiquement nazi ... tout entièrement marqué du sceau de la bassesse' ('an authentically nazi film, entirely marked by the stamp of baseness') and that it was more-over 'nul cinématographiquement parlant ... moralement hideux' ('cinematically rubbish ... and morally hideous' (Domarchi 1974: 66)). The general view from this camp seemed to be that the film was expressive of the worst excesses of vulgarity and sensation-alism in modern cinema, and that the only way to explain its popular success with the cinema-going public seemed to be to suggest, as did one reviewer in *Ecran*, that 'le succès du film classe aussi son public' ('the success of the film tells us a great deal about its public' (Domarchi 1974: 66)). Yet this was not a universal reaction, and the film was seen in other quarters as a revelation, where it was praised for its refreshing young actors and assured performances (Gérard Depardieu, Patrick Dewaere, Miou-Miou, confidently directed by Blier. The film has been regularly re-evaluated in the years that have followed, to the extent that it is now widely acknow-ledged as an important point of reference for contemporary French cinema. The significance of this film is that it first announced Blier's distinctive style to a wide public, and it is the bench-mark against which his other films have consistently been measured.

Calmos, released in 1975, was the subject of considerable and even more heated debate and controversy in the French press than *Les Valseuses*. Blier himself has looked back on it as 'un film raté comme il y en a toujours un dans la carrière d'un metteur en scène ... une sorte d'erreur de jeunesse' ('a real turkey, like there is in every director's career – a youthful error' (Haustrate 1988: 35)). Critics were fairly unanimous in their condemnation of what was seen as a misogynistic attack on the *MLF* (*Mouvement pour la Liberation de la Femme* – Women's Liberation Movement) and the events of the *Année de la Femme*, celebrated in 1975, and they expressed their views, often thinly veiled personal attacks on the director, vehemently in the press. The film, which was considerably more ambitious than the technical and financial means at Blier's disposal, was ultimately consigned to the same sort of oblivion as *Même si j'étais un espion*, and is today a work which goes largely uncommented upon in Blier's *œuvre*. Its interest for the spectator lies mainly in the way it approaches themes and dramatic codes which are common to Blier's earlier and later films, namely the experience of male fraternity, the notion of women as sexual predators, and the banality and functionality of sexual activity. In other ways, *Calmos* is an interesting example of just how far Blier misjudged the public mood in 1975: the graphic images of nudity and the depiction of sexual hysteria on the part of numerous female protagonists was perhaps inevitably read as an attack on contemporary political trends rather than the satirical allegory of gender relationships that Blier intended it to be.

In 1979 Bertrand Blier's fortunes turned around, and he received the Academy Award for Best Foreign Film for *Préparez vos mouchoirs* (1978), finding himself overnight in the esteemed company of such former recipients as Jacques Tati, François Truffaut and Luis Buñuel. The film, which reunited the Depardieu–Dewaere duo of *Les Valseuses* has a tight structure, witty dialogue and a clear line of comic development centred around notions of incongruity, and was praised by many critics. Some, however, remained troubled by what they continued to perceive as overtly misogynistic qualities in the screenplay and performances. This film pointed to Blier as an emerging *auteur*, with his own coherent style and favoured recurrent key themes, but its portrayal of female passivity at the service of sympathetic male leads, a development of the male–female relations in *Les Valseuses*, left it open to interpretation as expressive of a deep-rooted and unsavoury misogyny.

This was followed up in 1979 by *Buffet froid*, the film that finally saw a positive change in critical responses to Blier's work, and his acceptance as a 'serious' *auteur* by French film critics dates largely from the release of this film. The film was very different from those that had preceded it, all but eliminating a female presence to concentrate on a trio of male leads, and adopting a more fantastic quality in aspects of décor, characterisation and narrative logic. This embracing of an abstract dimension in a predominately comic framework was unusual in contemporary French production, and differentiated Blier from the mainstream of comic directors. It has been widely acknowledged as one of the most distinctive and important works both of the 1980s and of Blier's career. This film is a key one in any analysis of Blier's work, as it marks a definite turning point in his cinematic style, and shows a theatrical approach to dramatic conception which is based on substantially more than the informality and spontaneity of the *café-théâtre* performance, the generally acknowleged intertext of his earlier films. It is also notable, given the critical acclaim, for its surprising lack of commercial success, and for the setback that it eventually proved to be to Blier's subsequent film-making.

A fallow period ensued with Blier's films, not for the last time, ignored by the public. The first of these was *Beau-père* in 1981, a film adapted like *Les Valseuses* from Blier's own novel of the same name. The obvious departures in tone, genre and central characterisation set this film apart from its predecessors, and seemed to announce a new direction in Blier's work. Critics noted, often with some curiosity, the artistry of the film itself, commenting on, among other things, the successful first-time use of the cinemascope format, the elegance of the camerawork, and the close attention paid by Blier to interior shots and décor. These elements loaned intimate and claustrophobic qualities to the dramatic situation played out by Patrick Dewaere (acting without Depardieu for the first time in a Blier film) and the 14-year old actress Ariel Besse, in the role of his recently bereaved stepdaughter. *Beau-père*'s melodramatic premise, however, quickly revealed itself to be an unsettling pretext for further exploration of Blier's favoured themes and dramatic patterns: the film recaptures and inverts the provocative dramatic situation of *Préparez vos mouchoirs* where, at the instigation of the adolescent, a sexual relationship is formed between a mature woman and an adolescent boy. But, whereas in the earlier film, the contrast of the precociousness of the boy with the ineptitude of the adult males (Depardieu and Dewaere) was fruitful material for comic potential, the exploration of a quasi-incestuous relationship between an adult male and a precocious female adolescent laid Blier wide open to the accusation that his film was a further misogynistic 'fantasme de macho' ('macho fantasy' (*Cahiers du cinéma* 329, 1981: 63)), and the film was ultimately among Blier's least successful with the cinema-going public. Nevertheless, many critics supported the film, and it was selected to be presented at that year's Cannes festival.

Blier's next film was *La Femme de mon pote* (1983), a film which has been considerably underrated in the Blier corpus. Its main importance lies first in its interesting casting of the popular comedian Coluche, a star who had long expressed a desire to work with Blier, and second in the way in which it explores in an early, albeit relatively conventional way, the dramatic configuration of Blier's later film *Trop belle pour toi* (1989). Blier describes this first film as a 'demi-commande, avec carte blanche. La proposition était simplement de tourner un film avec Coluche. J'aimais Coluche. J'ai accepté' ('almost a commission, but with a free hand. The proposal was quite simply to make a film with Coluche. I liked Coluche, so I accepted' (Haustrate 1988: 59)). However, the working relationship between the two men proved to be extremely difficult, and neither was entirely satified with the result. Coluche's biographer Philippe Boggio notes that 'Le cinéaste reconnaîtra que ce film, par le comportement de Coluche, fut l'un des plus pénibles de sa carrière. "C'était un grand acteur, explique Bertrand Blier, mais qui refusait de jouer le jeu. D'apprendre son texte par exemple. Or, chez moi, les films sont très écrits"' (Boggio

1991: 375).[6] In the same text Coluche's co-star, Thierry Lhermitte, is quoted as saying 'Blier est hyperdirigiste ... il a besoin qu'on lui fasse confiance. Coluche était incapable de donner ça. Ça a explosé le premier jour'. ('Blier is a control freak ... he needs you to trust him. Coluche couldn't do that. They got off to a bad start right away.') The film had a huge budget ('presque hollywoodienne', 'almost Hollywood-size' (Haustrate 1988: 59)), no doubt benefited from the considerable celebrity of Coluche, and was a moderate commercial success, but it has since been relegated to the status of minor film in Blier's work. However, the film's anticipation of, and experimentation with the same dramatic and thematic inversions which underlie one of Blier's most successful films, *Trop belle pour toi*, point to this as an important film in Blier's evolving dramatic conception, and one which merits further consideration in any analysis of his work.

This first commissioned film was quickly followed by a second, *Notre histoire* starring Alain Delon and Nathalie Baye, a film which again had little commercial success. This film has never been fiercely defended by the director, who felt that conditions of production meant that it was far too rushed for it ever to be either good or successful, but critics have argued that it has been, along with *La Femme de mon pote*, severely underestimated in his work. Views ranged from vitriolic to lukewarm, acknowledging that this was an adventurous, if incomplete work from the director. This film is above all important for the place it holds in Blier's evolving thematic conception as 'le premier volet de ce triptyque sur les accidents et les folies de l'amour que viendront compléter *Tenue de soirée* (1985) et *Trop belle pour toi* (1989)' ('the first instalment of three reflections on the ups and downs of love that would be completed by *Tenue de soirée* and *Trop belle pour toi*' (Siclier 1991: 275)) and Blier has stated that elements of the film *Trop belle pour toi* were established and elaborated in this earlier work (Audé and

---

6 'The director was to admit that Coluche's behaviour made this one of the most difficult films of his career. "He was a great actor" Blier explains "but he refused to play the game. To learn his script for example. But my films are tightly scripted".'

Jeancolas 1989: 7).[7] Dramatically, the film furthers Blier's characteristic experimentation with casting known actors in roles which
are largely against type, and stylistically, it recalls and anticipates
the absurdist narrative forms and 'veine cauchemardesque'
('nightmarish qualities' (Toubiana 1986: 6)) of the more successful films *Buffet froid*, *Tenue de soirée* and *Trop belle pour toi*, as well
as the films from the most recent phase of Blier's career.

Critical and commercial success finally returned to Blier with
the release of the film *Tenue de soirée* in 1986. *Tenue de soirée* was
the sixth most popular film of 1986, beaten only in terms of
French production by Berri's hugely successful nostalgia vehicles
Jean de Florette and *Manon des sources*. Returning to his previously
successful formula of a trio of characters (Depardieu, Miou-Miou
and Michel Blanc, the actor replacing the original choice of
Dewaere who had committed suicide in July 1982), and thus a
dramatic reprise of the characters from *Les Valseuses*, Blier's film
was praised as the work of a mature *auteur* whose creativity and
influence in modern French cinema was now beyond doubt. On
the one hand, this was a film which subverted the boulevard
conventions of domestic love triangles, and challenged spectators
with some of the most dramatically daring roles in recent French
cinema. On the other, its focus, in terms of content, on the
portrayal of homosexual seduction, hedonistic criminality, and
incidences of physical and emotional aggression ensured that it
stood apart from the other major successes of the day.

Trop belle pour toi followed on from the success of *Tenue de
soirée*, was well received by critics and public alike, and received
more industry awards than any of Blier's previous or subsequent
films. This film, the biggest-grossing domestic film of 1989, arguably represents the *apogée* of Blier's career. For the critics of *Positif*
the importance of this film lay in the fact that 'pour la première
fois le cinéaste postule l'intégrité des personnages féminins' ('for
the first time the director advocates the integrity of female
characters' (Audé 1989: 5)) and it was widely perceived as marking

---

7 'Je suis parti sur un thème qui était un peu dans *Notre histoire* et qui est la raison
d'être du film' ('I based it on a theme that was already in *Notre histoire* and which
became the *raison d'être* of the film').

a significant development in both Blier's thematic base and his male-gendered approach to questions of emotion, sexuality and relationships. The film also signalled a new direction in Blier's approach to dialogue and *mise-en-scène*, and displayed more overtly dramatic and literary influences than the films that had preceded it. Interestingly, *Trop belle pour toi* is possibly the best known of Blier's films outside France, and it is arguably the film that has most contributed to Blier's status abroad as an 'art-house' director.

Merci la vie, the much awaited follow-up in 1991 to the successful *Trop belle pour toi* confirmed Blier's intention, hinted at earlier in his career, to focus on female rather than male protagonists (Haustrate 1988: 27).[8] The film, which featured a leading duo of two female stars (Anouk Grinberg and Charlotte Gainsbourg), combined elements of the buddy and road-movie genres, and was a clear thematic reprise of *Les Valseuses*.[9] In this first of a series of three films featuring the actress Anouk Grinberg, Blier furthered his now distinctive stylistic rupture with patterns of narrative coherence, and entered more fully into an experimental vein with regard to the temporal and spatial dimensions of his narratives. The film was well liked by critics, for whom it facilitated a re-evaluation of *Les Valseuses* and its enduring qualities of energy and insolence, and was very well received by the public, being the fifth most successful French film of 1991, behind a string of popular French comedies. Most interestingly of all, in spite of the very provocative performance of Grinberg and the controversial *mise-en-scène* of the woman as bearer of diseased sexuality, the misogynistic label which had dogged Blier's career seemed paradoxically – at least in some quarters – to have finally been put to rest: 'Misogyne, Blier? Allons donc. Misanthrope, plutôt. Tendance Molière'. ('Blier a misogynist? No way. More of a misanthropist. Molière style' (Heymann 1991: 13)).

8 'J'aimerais sortir du duo masculin. J'ai la velléité de concevoir un film qui mettrait en scène un duo de femmes. Il y a trop de tandems d'hommes dans le cinéma français.' ('I'd like to get away from the male duo. I'm inclined to create a film with a female duo. There are far too many male couples in French films.')

9 Guy Austin perceptively argues the case for *Les Valseuses* as intertext in *Merci la vie* (Austin 1994: 73–84).

After *Merci la vie*, *Un deux trois soleil* (1994) continued to point to a new social dimension in Blier's mature film-making, but this deeper foray into contemporary themes such as immigration, unemployment, social unrest and life in the inner city had a mixed success with critics and the public. Nevertheless, for Blier, this is an important film that is part of a concerted attempt to invest his film-making with a more personal dimension than ever before. In an interview at the time of the release of this film, he stated that: 'Je suis entré dans ma seconde carrière. Sur ces deux derniers films [*Merci la vie*, *Un deux trois soleil*] je me suis davantage impliqué en tant qu'individu' ('I've begun my second career. I've invested more of myself in these last two films' (Vecchi 1993: 26)). The film is significant in its furtherance of the dramatic scope of *Merci la vie*, engaging even more forcefully with a dynamic physical performance on the part of the central protagonists, and situating the narrative within the epic parameters of a woman's lifetime, covering a period from childhood to motherhood. The film is also marked by a dramatic interrogation of mortality, a device that furthers Blier's distinctive anti-realist approach to *mise-en-scène*, but also points to a poignant personal attempt to come to terms with the recent death of his father, Bernard (France Culture 1995).[10]

Mon homme (1996) is Blier's most recent film (as this book goes to press), and again features the actress Anouk Grinberg in the central role. The film is thematically consistent with the large majority of Blier's previous films, and has proved equally controversial in its depiction of female sexuality as a destabilising force in male–female relations. The highly stylised tableaux format, and the exploration of explicit processes of commentary and temporal disjunction that dominate in this film, are proof of a consistency of approach to narrative construction in Blier's later work, as well as of a continuing desire to invest his film-making with an unambiguously dramatic frame of reference. This film is

10 At Blier's own admission, the fantastic elements of this film are evidence of his desire to explore the power of cinema to 'defeat' death. He has acknowledged that 'ce film est marqué par la mort de mon père' ('My father's death has left its mark on this film' (France Culture 1995)).

also notable for its forceful intertextual dimension, which amounts, as we shall see, to a dialogue between Blier the film-maker of the 1990s, and the Blier of the earlier periods. *Mon homme* succeeds as a showcase of the content and techniques of the previous films, but also as an auto-commentary on the evolution in Blier's own aesthetic practices. The film is, more than any other, a vehicle for nostalgia, for review of an *œuvre*, and its melancholic comedy suggests that this film might be read as Blier's break with cinema in favour of other creative pursuits: 1997 saw the production at the Théâtre de la Porte-Saint-Martin of Blier's first play, *Les Côtelettes*, starring Philippe Noiret and Michel Bouquet. This was followed by the publication in 1998 of Blier's third novel *Existe en blanc*, a caustic account of fetishisation and its consequences.

Categories and types of films

It is difficult to assign labels in a body of work as eclectic and wilfully ludic as Blier's, because part of the purpose of this director is to create films which, in their formal construction, defy all attempts at generic classification. Blier combines realism with spectacle (*Hitler, connais pas!*), comedy with tragedy (*Merci la vie*), intimate drama with abstraction (*Trop belle pour toi*) and melo-drama with burlesque (*Tenue de soirée*). His approach to form is that of *bricolage* (the 'melting-pot' approach), based on the concept of 'cultural collision', or what in Bakhtinian terms we might call a dialogical interaction between the high and the low in cultural expression. These fusions of generic forms and conventions – frequently conflictual, but always productive – have the effect of disconcerting the potentially uncritical viewer through the chal-lenge that they mount to expectations about representation. As Blier has stated:

> Dès mon travail de préparation, j'envisage les procédés qui vont me permettre de surprendre. J'aime, en particulier, utiliser les poncifs ou les structures dramatiques classiques en m'en servant de base. Puis je les retourne comme un gant. Ça casse les émotions,

ça brise le confort intellectuel dans lequel le spectateur se croyait installé. (Haustrate 1988: 115)[11]

Comfortable viewing, where one succumbs to the illusion and is compelled into a state of empathetic identification by the diegesis and narrative development, is, then, the very antithesis of Blier's cinematic conception. His films typically begin *in medias res*, tend towards elliptical narration and character inconsistency, and are ultimately frustratingly inconclusive for the spectator who would make sense of the 'story'. The frequently cyclical nature of the narratives adds to the creation of the atmosphere of defamiliarisation and vague incoherence that is so characteristic of Blier's cinematic world.

But if we were to focus instead on the notion of thematic and stylistic tendencies that are common to the films, then it is possible to locate them in three distinct categories, which in turn reflect the three broad periods and narrative approaches in Blier's work. Such an approach has the added advantage of allowing us to trace the most significant developments in his cinematic conception from the early period to his most recent work. The first category is that of the often bawdy comedies, essentially of his early career, which rely on the easy camaraderie and sexual fraternity of duos of male characters, and which document the largely picaresque itinerary of this genre's classically ambivalent heroes. These films (*Les Valseuses*, *Calmos*, *Préparez vos mouchoirs*, *Buffet froid*, *La Femme de mon pote* and *Tenue de soirée*) all privilege male relationships, and explore the nature of masculinity and male identity within a predominantly comic framework. The casting in these films is interesting: Gérard Depardieu appears in four of the films, and Dewaere,[12] Miou-Miou, Jean-Pierre Marielle

11 'From the beginning, I try to identify strategies that will let me take the viewer by surprise. I'm particularly fond of using clichés and classic dramatic forms as my starting point. Then I completely reverse them. It upsets the emotional balance, shatters the cocoon of intellectual comfort in which spectators have hoped to bury themselves.'

12 Blier long had Dewaere in mind for a third role, that of Antoine in *Tenue de soirée*, but this was completed after his death with Michel Blanc in the role. Similarly, the role of Solange in *Préparez vos mouchoirs* (taken by Carole Laure) was originally intended for Miou-Miou.

and Bernard Blier each appear in two of the films. This dramatic notion of permutation is a key stylistic component of Blier's art, and is one to which we shall return. Of note here is that the relationships performed by the duos Depardieu–Dewaere, Rochefort–Marielle, Coluche–Lhermitte can all be read as variations on a type: one partner handsome, egotistical and sexually demanding, the other more physically robust, relatively altruistic, and who exerts an authority over the actions and emotions of the first. The relationships frequently display a triangular dimension, either by the incorporation of a third male (Jean Carmet in *Buffet froid*), or more commonly in the presence of a female companion who forms a key, but secondary component of the social unit. This casting has led to readings of Blier's films as vehicles for female marginalisation and exclusion, but as the discussion in Chapter 4 of this book makes clear, this is only part of the picture, and such an interpretation ignores the question of the importance of female performance in Blier's work.

The second group of films are the less explicitly comic films (*Hitler connais pas!*, *Même si j'étais un espion*, *Beau-père*, *Notre histoire*, and *Trop belle pour toi*), with which, excepting *Trop belle pour toi*, Blier enjoyed only moderate commercial success. The films are similar in their establishing of a cerebral and reflective, rather than physical mode of being, wherein the main protagonists express a degree of alienation with regard to a complex moral dilemma, which dominates in their lives. This group of films attempts to deal with the complexities and dynamics of social, rather than purely sexual interaction, and is increasingly constructed around principles of ambiguity, abstraction and narrative fragmentation. Inasmuch as there is a common pattern, the films broadly document a shift in focus from the group, to intimate one-to-one male–female relationships, through to a reliance on what has often been considered his forte, the triangular relationship. As we shall see in Chapter 3, the trio for Blier represents a distillation of the concept of community interaction, and it is with this dramatic configuration that he has arguably done his most original work.

The third category of films is that of Blier's mature career, or what Blier himself has termed his 'seconde carrière' ('second career'). These films, from the 1990s (*Merci la Vie*, *Un deux trois soleil* and *Mon homme*), all feature the actress Anouk Grinberg, and are characterised first by their central focus on female protagonists, and second by their very active exploration of the cinematic limitations of female representation and performance. Alongside this, Blier's narratives engage – although not always successfully – with issues of contemporary social significance such as Aids, racism, and 'fracture sociale' (social breakdown). These fragmented digressive narratives ultimately have little to say about important social topics, allowing form to dominate over content, such that the way of telling becomes of more interest to the viewer than the telling itself. This discussion will be taken up in Chapter 5.

The categories outlined above are, of course, overlapping and to a large extent unstable groupings, constructed to allow us to manoeuvre within and between the wide body of work in question here; they are therefore open to challenge. What is not in doubt, however, is that Blier's work has displayed from the earliest days until his most recent work a great consistency in thematic and stylistic features. There are three principal thematic concerns which recur in the films: first, all the films, without exception, depict the difficulty of communication – sexual and social – between the sexes. This approach to male–female relationships – depicted variously in terms of incomprehension (*Les Valseuses*), all-out war (*Calmos*), same-sex solidarity (*Tenue de soirée*) and overpowering desire (*Trop belle pour toi*) – has contributed to Blier's reputation for misogyny outlined above, and has left him for a long time branded as an ideologically suspect film-maker.

Second, Blier's work expresses a consistent and recurrent desire to inhabit social groups and structures, albeit in units which appear to deviate from the social norm. As suggested above, Blier's heroes never operate in isolation, but rather, somewhat in the tradition of 1950s absurd theatre, exist in patterns of interdependence which the protagonists have no desire to abandon, no matter how problematic the relationships. Indeed, the desire expressed by the characters to live in the company of others, in micro-communities which, in this case, sanction unrestrained physical and emotional intercourse is reminiscent of the 'utopian urge' of revolutionary discourse, and as such is a profoundly liberating impulse in the films. The physical manifestation of these communities is the choreographed action of multiple figures which is such a feature of the comic films in particular. These images, which encapsulate visually the artificial eloquence of rhetorical exchange that underpins the dialogue of all Blier's films, are evidence of a highly original approach to the question of performance in modern French cinema.

Third, the films all mount an attack on notions of bourgeois morality and convention. The function of Blier's particular brand of *dérision* is to 'épater les bourgeois' ('shock the middle classes'), and this is achieved through his confrontation of 'taboo subjects' (sexual promiscuity, homosexuality, transvestism and adolescent sexuality to name but the most striking), his enthusiasm for verbal and pictorial vulgarity, and the *mise-en-scène* of liberated sexuality. This tendency is not peculiar to Blier. Indeed, the oppositional comic attacks and biting satire of contemporary mores which we find in his films can be fundamentally located within an established French tradition of satire of which Rabelais is simply one of the earliest exponents, and are intrinsically bound up with the popular modern manifestation of this in the subversive popular cultural apparatus which anticipated, commented upon, and gave momentum to much of the mood of post–1968 popular French culture. Blier's adaptation of elements of these popular subversive forms into a cinematic expression, and the very innovative and self-conscious interrogation of the popular in subject-matter, language, characterisation and narrative forms which this entailed, was, in the 1970s, distinctive and original in French cinema, but was also, given its characteristic lack of subtlety and rejection of aesthetic conventions, something which, unsurprisingly, the critics and public alike found difficult to evaluate.

Stylistic features

Blier's films share a body of stylistic features which are consistent from film to film. The tendency to construct language, action and characterisation in terms of group action, aggression and transgression results in an overarching anarcho-comic system of images and words which can best be defined as 'festive-ludic'. Indeed, Blier's extensive use of techniques of inversion, reversal and subversion with regard to physical characterisation, character behaviour, speech content, and the rules of dramatic and social logic is, as stated above, consistent with that observed by Mikhail Bakhtin in *Rabelais and his World*. The transgressive, and often explicitly deviant characters are types that are repeated from film to film, and this is intensified in Blier's repeated selection of key actors over the body of work. Generically, his films display affinities with the literary genre that Bakhtin has identified as 'grotesque realism', wherein a conflict is apparent between popular cultural forms of expression and classical aesthetics. Blier's grotesque operates on a visual as well as a verbal level, and is informed by the same principle of 'degradation' as that identified by Bakhtin in the medieval carnival rites.

Furthermore, Blier's diegetic world, although resolutely contemporary, and immediately recognisable as either urban or rural modern France is an absurd world (in the philosophical sense of the word) where all is prey to 'distortions fantastiques' ('fantastic distortions'). As Pascal Bonitzer points out, Blier's films display 'une véritable gourmandise à convoquer tous les lieux, les corps, les êtres, les pensées, les objets les plus sinistres de la petite-bourgeoisie française' ('a real gluttony for portraying all the places, forms, beings, thoughts, and most sinister objects of the French lower-middle classes' (Bonitzer 1984: 105)). The sense of disorientation expressed by the characters and experienced by the viewer of a Blier film is compounded by the realisation that what we see before us should be wholly usual and untroubling. This collision between a familiar iconographical frame of reference and the artificiality of front-of-stage performance, creates a *Verfremdungseffekt* (alienation effect) similar to that identified by Bertolt Brecht in relation to Epic theatre.[13]

---

13 The 'alienation effect' is the term used in theatre to describe the process whereby the spectator is prevented from establishing too empathetic an

The form of the films is our final area of stylistic interest. Blier's films are about the difficulties as well as the possibilities of narration/storytelling. The films very crucially do not engage with a realist mode of film-making, but instead are distinctive in that they frequently display the formal qualities of fable or parable, or indeed the stand-up sketch common to the *café-théâtre*.[14] They frequently have an abstract and at times fantastic dimension to their narrative construction, and make use of a rhetorical narrative framework in performance. Plot is frequently subordinated to elaborate set pieces in which a form of verbal jousting takes place between characters, or between a character and the spectator: dialogue is often classically stichomythic, with disputes between characters expressed in patterns of antithesis and rhetorical repetition (see for example the opening scene of *Buffet froid* or the central dinner scene in *Tenue de soirée*); circumlocution and hyperbole are common features of verbal discourse (*Calmos, Préparez vos mouchoirs*), and characters all too frequently transgress the diegetic logic of the film to address the spectator, or query some element of narrative development (*Trop belle pour toi, Merci la vie*). This deliberately non-realist approach is quite unusual in modern French cinema, and can be interpreted as partly a reaction to comfortable viewing, partly an endeavour to engage with the Godardian tendency in modern cinema to deconstruct the inherent complexities of elements of narration. As one critic has put it:

> Blier se moque ... du dogme qui veut qu'une bonne histoire, au cinéma, puisse se résumer en une phrase ... En réalité, il ne raconte pas d'histoire, il aligne des scènes en essayant d'épuiser la logique de chacune des situations, de chacun des êtres qu'il met en place. (Bonitzer 1984: 106)[15]

---

identification with characters and action on stage, through being kept aware of the processes of illusion which traditionally surround dramatic expression.

14 Geneviève in *Calmos* makes a reference to the 'jolie fable' ('wonderful tale') of which the characters are a part.

15 'Blier mocks the dogma which says that in the cinema, a good story can be summed up in a single sentence. ... In fact, he doesn't tell a story, he puts scenes side by side and attempts to exhaust the logic of each of the situations, of each of the characters within it'.

Blier's place in the contemporary industry

Given Blier's tendency to create films which go against the representational norms of mainstream commercial cinema, how might
we understand and assess his contribution to the modern French
industry? A starting point might be to look at Blier's work in terms
of those with whom he has collaborated, and the distinctive
performance style that he has fostered in his work. Blier was one
of the first directors to work with the new generation of actor-
comedians emerging in the 1970s from Parisian *café-théâtre*, most
notably Miou-Miou, Patrick Dewaere, Michel Blanc and Josiane
Balasko. *Les Valseuses* was the film that effectively launched Gérard
Depardieu's career, and Blier and the star have frequently collaborated since, with Blier providing Depardieu with some of his
most memorable roles and acting as co-producer for a number of
Depardieu's films. His films were vehicles for 'discovering' many
of today's cinema's new stars and created challenging roles, often
cast against established type, for those already well known, among
them Michel Serrault, Jean Carmet, Nathalie Baye, Alain Delon,
Marcello Mastroianni, Anouk Grinberg, Thierry Lhermitte and
Coluche. Bertrand Blier has ultimately been a key figure and
influence in the process of renewal that has informed French
cinema since the beginning of the 1970s, exploring and promoting
new comic and dramatic trends, and facilitating the emergence of
the popular comic cinematic forms that have been a feature of the
great majority of commercial and popular box-office hits of the
1980s and 1990s. *Cahiers du cinéma* recently described him as 'le
père géniteur et spirituel de cette famille comique' ('the father and
spiritual adviser to this family of comics' (Strauss 1995: 60)),
pointing to the considerable influence that Blier has exerted on
the group of actors and directors who are today at the forefront of
innovation in French film comedy.

A second place we might look to is the content of Blier's films:
Blier's work is important in that it reflects, and to some extent can
be said to document, the evolution in social habits and youth
culture in post–1968 France. The cynical, anarchic yet spontaneous and exuberant *Les Valseuses* was a landmark film in French
cinema history, revealing the possibilities of expression for the

popular consciousness, or what modern popular theatre has termed the *'non-public'*.[16] The commercial and popular success of this film was such that it quickly acquired the status of a *'coup médiatique'* ('media event'), a totem film in the year's French production. Attempting to explain the importance of this film to a generation of aspiring young actors and directors, as well as to a youth audience in general terms, Josiane Balasko recounts:

> Pour nous, le film a été un choc en 73, l'équivalent pour ceux qui, à l'âge de vingt ans, ont vu *A bout de souffle*. D'un seul coup, on se reconnaissait, on voyait des personnages proches de nous, qui parlaient un langage à la fois simple et stylisé, sophistiqué, mais qui passait très bien. (Toubiana 1988: 14)[17]

And, again, Miou-Miou expresses her understanding of the film's popularity in terms of the sheer authenticity of the performers:

> Au cinéma, on prend un malin plaisir à dépeindre les apprenties, les 'travailleuses' comme des filles tristes, grisailles. Les stars qui les interprètent s'amusent à s'enlaidir et à faire de la 'composition' ... C'est la première fois que dans un film, on nous montrait telles que nous sommes. (Douin 1976)[18]

Finally, what is highly significant in Blier's work is the way in which it has incorporated into modern film-making not only the iconoclastic elements and general subversive tone promoted by the pre- and post–1968 counter-culture, but more particularly, the way in which it has explored the close association between innovative modern film-making and the expressive modes of modern French mainstream theatrical culture and practice. Arguably,

---

16 The *'non-public'* was the term coined by Jean Vilar to identify those denied access to participation in mainstream cultural activities such as theatre, on grounds of class, education, finance and location.

17 'For us in 1973, the film was a complete shock, as was Godard's *Breathless* for those who saw it at the age of twenty All of a sudden, there we were on the screen, characters just like us, who spoke simply but with sophistication and style, in a way that worked.'

18 'In films, directors take great pleasure in showing working women as miserable, drab types. The stars who play these parts love making themselves ugly, love "getting into the part". It was the first time ever that a film showed us just as we were.'

Blier's greatest originality as a film-maker lies in the self-conscious use he makes in his film-making of the forms and content of popular drama in a way that seeks to highlight rather than disguise the patterns of transference and influence. Blier's work is innovative and important in the context of modern French cinema in that it demonstrates an awareness, and reflects a new understanding of the language of French popular theatre, engaging with experimental dramatic forms of the type explored in modern French Brechtian-influenced theatre, in particular *création collective*, as well as in alternative counter-cultural forms. As we shall see, an analysis of the dramatic base of Blier's work reveals a considered approach to the question of traditional popular spectacle in a range of modern manifestations, and goes some way to explaining the cultural context within which he operates.

References

Audé, Françoise (1989), 'Belle pour moi (Trop belle pour toi)', *Positif*, May.

Audé, Françoise and Jeancolas, Jean-Pierre (1989) 'Entretien avec Bertrand Blier', *Positif*, May.

Austin, Guy (1994), 'History and Spectacle in Blier's *Merci la vie*', *French Cultural Studies*, 5, 73–84.

Boggio, Philippe (1991), *Coluche*, Paris, J'ai lu/Flammarion.

Bonitzer, Pascal (1984), 'Quelle histoire?', *Cahiers du cinéma* 360–1, summer, 104–6.

Cahiers du cinéma (1981), '*Beau-père*', 329, November.

Domarchi, Jean (1974), '*Les Valseuses*', *Ecran* 25, May.

Douin, Jean-Luc (1976), 'Entretien avec Miou-Miou', *Télérama* 1359, 28 January, 60–1.

France Culture (1995) 'Le bon plaisir de Bertrand Blier', broadcast 18 February.

Haustrate, Gaston (1988), *Bertrand Blier*, Paris, Edilig.

Hauttecœur, J.-P. (1963), 'Hitler, connais pas ...', *La Croix*, 10 August.

Heymann, Danièle (1991), 'A elles la liberté', *Le Monde (Arts et spectacle)*, 14 March.

Jeancolas, Jean-Pierre (1979), *Le Cinéma des Français: La Vème République (1958–1978)*, Paris, Editions Stock.

Jeander (1963), 'Hitler, connais pas!', *Libération*, 31 July.

Riou, Alain (1993), 'L'impossible Monsieur B. B ...', *Le Nouvel Observateur*, 19 August.

Siclier, Jacques (1991), *Le Cinéma français 2: de Baisers volés à Cyrano de Bergerac 1968–1990*, Paris, Ramsay.

Strauss, Frédéric (1995), 'L'empire des sens' *Cahiers du cinéma* 489, March.

Toubiana, Serge (1986), 'Le Cauchemar d'Antoine', *Cahiers du cinéma* 382, April.

Toubiana, Serge (1988) 'Josiane Balasko, Bertrand Blier: jeux de mots, jeux d'acteurs', *Cahiers du cinéma* 407–8, May.

Trémois, Claude-Marie (1974), '*Les Valseuses*', *Télérama* 1261, 16 March.

Tulard, Jean (1995), *Guide des films 1895–1995*, Vol. L–Z, Paris, Laffont.

Vecchi, Philippe (1993), 'J'aime les places où il n'y a pas un arbre', *Libération*, 18 August.

2

A cinema of the absurd

Dramatic style

The narrative structures of Blier's films vary from the episodic, frequently picaresque, yet largely linear *récits* of *Les Valseuses*, *Calmos*, *Préparez vos mouchoirs*, *Beau-père*, *La Femme de mon pote*, and *Tenue de soirée* to the more complex and digressive reflections of *Buffet froid*, *Notre histoire*, *Trop belle pour toi*, *Merci la vie*, *Un deux trois soleil* and *Mon homme*; *Même si j'étais un espion* and *Hitler connais pas!* are early experiments in each respective mode. Blier's progressive tendency in the corpus of his work has been away from the elliptical editing of the early comic films to a more generally abstract, stylised and self-referential cinematic form, which explicitly prioritises the elaboration of disruptive narrative devices. As a general principle, the narrative of both early and later films tends to be set in motion by a curious, yet uncomplicated dramatic event, which has no particular significance beyond the initial action of the film: in *Les Valseuses* a man is injured in the testicles and, with his friend, seeks ways to reassure himself that he is still virile; in *Préparez vos mouchoirs* a man's wife is unable to conceive and he asks a stranger in a restaurant to intervene to see if he can impregnate her in his place; in *Tenue de soirée* a couple down on their luck meet an ex-convict who changes their lives materially and seduces the husband in the process. In these films, there is little sense of a history extended before or beyond the events portrayed; the events themselves and what they construct within the plot duration are of more importance than any wider understanding of the characters and their dilemmas. In this way, the action of the film, including the events, the dialogue and the environment in which these are played out, constitute the principal focus for the spectator, who is provided with an absolute minimum of extraneous diegetic information. Spectatorial construction of the narrative draws for the most part on the information provided by the material visual and verbal elements of the film, and little on a perceived extra-diegetic dimension that is non-concretised in dramatic terms. Furthermore, the gradual abandonment of marks of temporal identification, both for characters and spectators, is expressive of a sense of the irrationality of human relationships and experience and Blier succeeds in generating moments of alienation and incomprehension, both in the content and form of his work. Dramatic incoherence is encoded and conveyed by the accumulation of scenes that frequently appear to have no clear causal link.

In formal terms, Blier's approach to narrative construction is a largely unconventional one; his approach runs counter to that which informs much classic narrative cinema which, as Susan Hayward has suggested 'tends to follow a fairly standard set of patterns which can be defined by the triads order/disorder/order and order/enigma/resolution' (Hayward 1996: 251). It is a characteristic, and characteristically disconcerting feature of Blier's work across the range of films, that the narratives typically do not commence in a state of order, nor do they set about determining a solution to the problems raised in the course of the events. Instead, the enigma is present from the outset of the action, a moment of order is frequently attained in the mid-section of the films, but this temporary attempt at conventional narrative resolution is then rejected as the films move towards a further puzzle or enigma. The absence of an initial sense of cause and effect in the opening scenes, into which the spectator intrudes *in medias res*, is compounded by the difficulty for the spectator of establishing subsequent patterns of cause and effect as the films progress; for example, the spectator never fully understands the nature of the three-way relationship between Pierrot, Jean-Claude and Marie-Ange in *Les Valseuses*, nor the motivation of Bob,

Antoine and Monique in *Tenue de soirée*, because the spectator is never given close access to the psychological information that would explain this. This is less problematic in the more linear texts indicated above, where the comic tone tends to reinforce the spectator's engagement with the narrative; *Préparez vos mouchoirs*, for example, dramatises the stages of obsession, not in the sense of a development from inception to resolution, but rather in terms of an ever-present driving force; this shared obsession is what the characters amount to, and every action and line of dialogue has a bearing on it. The film takes the spectator into an enclosed, very intimate, diegetic world wherein obsessions take on an increasingly extravagant multiple aspect: Solange's fertility, the male characters' love of Mozart, book collections, memory recall, and ultimately the role/presence of Christian and his sexuality are all the subject of a comic narrative focus. But the second series of films is characterised by a more ambiguous comedy which depends on the explicit and systematic undermining of patterns of causality and effect: a reversal of logical sequences is the structuring mechanism of *Buffet froid*, where the main characters seem to have as little information about the events in progress as the spectator; *Merci la vie* defies all attempts by characters and spectators alike to locate the action in terms of causal and temporal logic. Indeed, it is a feature of Blier's distinctive style that the films prioritise above all else a dramatic enactment of the effects of a given situation, however irrational or arbitrary this may be: thus scenes have their own value irrespective of their relationhip to what precedes or follows. This interest in situations and consequences, rather than solutions is a key aspect of Blier's work, and a deliberate dispensing with the illusion of linearity is both the method and the result of this approach.

One way of understanding the system of dramatic cohesion that unifies the action of Blier's films is to read it in terms of an 'absurdist' conception. In the 1950s, France witnessed a period of self-consciously experimental or avant-garde domestic drama, now commonly termed the *théâtre de l'absurde*. The experimental base of this school of theatre was represented most forcefully by the work of Samuel Beckett, Eugène Ionesco, Arthur Adamov and

Jean Genet, and the movement was unique in that its major exponents in France were mainly foreign writers and artists who had chosen to make a home for themselves in France. Martin Esslin, who coined the term 'Theatre of the Absurd', has identified the hallmarks of its style as follows:

> the abandonment of concepts of character and motivation; the concentration on states of mind and basic human situations, rather than on the development of a narrative plot from exposition to solution; the devaluation of language as a means of communication and understanding; the rejection of didactic purpose; and the confrontation of the spectator with the harsh facts of a cruel world and his own isolation. (Esslin 1972, 228)

The *théâtre de l'absurde*, then, expresses a sense of revolt with regard to conventional theatre practice, and constructs a new dramatic form based on the collision of elements: this revolt is also apparent in Blier's work, which explores a collision of tragic and comic genres, unpredictability in language and action, and privileges superficial or surface aspects of characterisation over psychological depth. Like the world created by the absurdist playwrights, freed from the constraints of causality and consequentiality, Blier's diegetic universe is also 'a world of infinite possibilities' (Bradby 1991: 77). The effect of this approach in the theatre is to undermine the traditional position of the spectator who, bound by illusion, follows a play via a process of empathetic identification, motivated by 'l'attente anxieuse de la fin' ('anxious anticipation of the ending' (Demarcy 1973: 329)). At the same time, the self-consciousness of form and wilful disruptiveness of the style amounts to an attitude of aggression towards the audience and its expectations. In the same way, the privileging of theatricality over any kind of mimetic realism, and the exploration of popular dramatic tropes such as non-linearity are central to Blier's stylistic approach, and explain some of what it is about his work that is confusing for viewers schooled in the realist comedy of manners so characteristic of French cinema. An association with a high literary theatrical form, which, according to popular perception one accesses through complex philosophical concepts, may seem to be at odds with Blier's marked popular style. Yet, as the above analysis shows, Blier's films display immediate and fundamental parallels with many of the dramatic features of the work of the absurdist playwrights, and thus such a contextualisation of his work is appropriate and entirely justified.

Indeed, the self-consciousness of form common to absurdist theatre, Brechtian theatre and the experimental forms such as *création collective* which succeeded these in France, finds an expression in Blier's *mise-en-scène* which is unusual in modern French cinema; in his films distortions of dramatic logic and of cinematic convention go hand in hand. As well as an attention to pace and repetition in the performance of 'ordinary behaviour', qualities of enactment and role-play are taken up by the actors in performance of their characters, conveying an artificiality which is at odds with an often hyper-naturalistic physical construction. Elsewhere Blier subverts cinematic conventions through such techniques as direct-to-camera verbal address, dramatic autocommentary (Beckett's 'we're not beginning to mean something?'), the integration of an interrogative spectator within the diegesis, and the drawing of attention to conventionally 'invisible' filmic devices. These disruptions of theatrical and cinematic conventions are used by Blier to create a fictional world which is anything but securely self-contained within illusory narrative norms. The disorientation and confusion provoked by content are thus intensified in the narrative form which continually disrupts our spectatorial position, thereby confirming our perception of Blier's world as unpredictable and governed by rules of logic which are entirely arbitrary.

The diegetic world

The subversive approach to the notion of the dramatic catalyst is somewhere we might usefully begin to conduct a detailed analysis of Blier's style. In almost all cases the immediate focus of the film is on the banal activity of social or domestic life – boredom (*Les Valseuses*; *Calmos*; *Beau-père*; *Notre histoire*; *Tenue de soirée*), morning routines (*La Femme de mon pote*; *Un deux trois soleil*), waiting

(*Calmos*; *Buffet froid*; *Trop belle pour toi*; *Mon homme*), quarrels (*Tenue de soirée*; *Merci la vie*). This represents a conventional order of sorts (see above, p. 31), but this is quickly undermined by a comic moment based on incongruity: an unexpected intrusion, a surprising verbal intervention, a shocking physical action. We, like the characters around whom the action unfolds, find ourselves in a diegetic world where the unpredictable will become the clearest point of reference.

As the films develop, we note the reduced cast with which Blier works: all films focus on a limited number of central subjects, most typically groups of two or three characters. These recurrent dramatic configurations facilitate the ritualised performance of routine action and allow social interaction to take on an almost choreographed aspect. The casting of characters as outcasts, potential or actual deviants, as individuals on the margins of their society is typical of absurd theatre's approach to characterisation. Here as there, the characters are potentially tragic figures whose potentially tragic existence, but not their intrinsic humanity, is constantly challenged by a comic treatment which highlights their essential ambiguity. The scatological dialogue, co-ordinated behaviour and capacity for self-interrogation all testify to this.

The repetition of key images and actions that this entails creates a series of constant features that allow the viewer to overcome the intrinsic incoherence of the narrative, while paradoxically reinforcing a sense of the dramatic stasis at the heart of absurdist performance: these are films in which, for all their apparent dynamism, no one goes anywhere, forward movement is severely restricted, circularity is the dominant mode of propulsion. These 'constants' often work to intensify the comic tone, itself a powerful device for re-engaging the spectator with the narrative. In *Les Valseuses*, the two male characters become mirror images of each other, performing parallel actions, and wearing identical clothes; in *Préparez vos mouchoirs* there is a suggestion of costumes which gains dramatic momentum as each of the males involved in a sexual relationship with Solange is seen to wear a turtleneck jumper which she has knitted; in *Notre histoire* Robert Avranche returns frequently to a source point: an armchair. This technique is extended by Blier to an intertextual system of images across the corpus of his work: images like the shopping trolley in the opening scenes of *Les Valseuses* and *Merci la vie*, or scenes like that of the burglary phlegmatically dismissed by the bourgeois proprietor (played by Jean Rochefort) in *Tenue de soirée* and *Un deux trois soleil*, films separated by on the one hand nearly twenty years and on the other eight years, are evidence of a pattern of dramatic repetition and reworking of elements, and of a conscious attempt at intertextuality. This accumulation of images and of systems of reference within and across films, constitutes a process of direct address to the spectator, inviting us to collaborate with the film-maker and artists about the essential artifice of the mode of representation.

The pace of the performance in the films points to the influence of an absurdist conception on Blier's work, where we find the same aspects of accumulation, proliferation, and rapidity as in many of Eugène Ionesco's plays.[1] One example of how Blier expresses a similar pattern of transference of inner anxieties onto the dramatic environment is observable in the multiplication of locales. These fall into three categories: similar (this can take place within a single film such as *Tenue de soirée* in which a series of very similar grand houses are burgled by the central characters, or across a series of films such as *Les Valseuses*, *Préparez vos mouchoirs*, *Buffet froid* which each use an isolated rural cottage as a key locale); sinister (the deserted quality of the RER station in the opening scene of *Buffet froid* is echoed throughout the film in locales such as the *parvis de la tour*, the empty appartments and streets, even the silent countryside); labyrinthine (such as the office space divided by glass partitions in *Trop belle pour toi* or the vast HLMs (tower blocks) of *Un deux trois soleil*). These devices create for the spectator a similar sense of disorientation to that experienced or expressed by the characters in these films.

The visual incongruity or collision of elements common to absurdist theatre is present on a wide visual and aural scale in Blier's work. It is frequently the case that a setting displays

1 These features are characteristic of the treatment of both language and material elements in Ionesco's *Les Chaises*, *Rhinocéros* and *La Leçon*.

qualities which are culturally distinct from the action to which it serves as a background. In *Les Valseuses*, for instance, the scene of Marie-Ange's orgasm takes place against an idyllic painterly tableau of a riverside, which, complemented by the dress of the male characters, is forcefully reminiscent of Renoir's *Une partie de campagne* (1936), and inevitably invites a further level of inter-textual reference, that of Auguste Renoir's Impressionist paintings. The dialogue between Jean-Claude and Pierrot which overlies this shot is, however, banal in the extreme, and the sounds of Marie-Ange's orgasm disturb the tranquillity profoundly, as do the actions of the frustrated male observers. A similar effect is present in a subsequent scene where a recently stolen car is cursed – 'espèce de putain de bagnole de merde' ('bloody crappy car') – in front of a backdrop of flower fields of stunning beauty. In *Tenue de soirée*, the pimping of short, unattractive, vulnerable Antoine takes place against a background of graceful, elegant statues of naked men, and the salaciousness of the bourgeois who demand an orgy of their housebreakers is entirely at odds with the quiet, ethereal beauty of their material environment. *Mon homme* explores a collision between the divine and the profane in its portrayal of the intimacy of Marie and Jeannot: the divine image suggested by the tramp's long hair, beard and status as an outcast is taken up in the quasi-religious music that dominates the scene, and in Marie's actions as a good Samaritan offering her body to the outcast. The sacred qualities of this highly charged, highly erotic scene, are however rapidly undermined by the close-up image of the tramp's hands like satanic claws on Marie's perfect skin, and by the sudden movement away from apparently ritualised behaviour to something closer to sado-masochistic dominance. These collisions are highy effective dramatic devices which enhance the complex-ities established by patterns of contradiction and opposition in Blier's characters (see below, pp. 47–56).

Techniques of disruption

Direct verbal address to the camera is one of Blier's most favoured and widely used devices, and was the cinematic technique that began his career. It is implicit in the majority of his titles which express an imperative (*Calmos, Préparez vos mouchoirs*), a statement (*Hitler connais pas!, Merci la vie, Mon homme*) or an opinion (*Trop belle pour toi*) directed at another party. *La Femme de mon pote, Notre histoire, Un deux trois soleil* are all evocative of the verbal mode, as are the use of terms such as '*les valseuses*' ('bollocks'), which are more usually spoken than written. Blier's films are therefore conceived of not as objective creations, designed to remain on the screen and be viewed passively at a safe distance, but rather as exchanges with the spectator, where he or she is cajoled into a critical exchange, appealed to as a complicit participant in the ongoing action.

Blier first experimented with this technique in *Hitler, connais pas!*, in which he used the narrative mechanism of the interview to allow eleven young people to talk about themselves and their experiences, filming them direct to camera, mostly in close shot, as they responded to unheard questions on the part of the interviewer-director. The film at first appears to have ethnographic intentions consistent with the *cinéma-vérité* mode of film-making, exploring the views and preoccupations of a representative group of individuals, allowing its subjects to locate themselves, their emotions and their attitudes to life with respect to the various conditions of their lives. As the film progresses, the intercutting of the monologues according to specific subject areas (family relationships, ambitions, lifestyles) creates the impression of a conversation taking place between the assembled youths: one delinquent character begins to talk about his mother's life; another young man from the *Assistance Publique* announces 'je n'ai pratiquement pas connu mes parents' ('I barely knew my parents'); a young single mother, who has told us that she is the eldest of ten children replies 'ma mère a quarante-quatre ans' ('my mother is forty-four'). 'Ma mère s'est réfugiée' ('my mother just took off'), says the second young man, and again the young woman adds a comment about her own mother. The conversation, however, is entirely inauthentic, for as Blier makes very clear in the inter-title that prefaces the film

Il s'agit uniquement de onze jeunes qui ont, ou qui vont avoir, vingt ans en 1963. Onze personnages c'est tout ... choisis dans le but de faire un spectacle et non une enquête. Bien que le tournage les rapproche, ils ne se sont jamais rencontrés pendant le tournage.[2]

Indeed, Blier's working method on this film was as follows: he recorded interviews with twelve selected young people over a period of twelve days, keeping them isolated from each other in order to eliminate any possibility of eventual filmed reaction influenced by actual experience. Eleven were finally retained for the film and Blier worked on these eleven recordings, examining the words and images of his interviewees, focusing on the idea of carrying out 'du montage sur les visages' ('montage on faces') and engineering 'des conversations artificielles entre les gens qui ne s'étaient jamais vus' ('artificial conversations between people who had never actually met' (Haustrate 1988: 13)). Temporal and spatial unity was achieved by a long process of montage, which saw the disparate fragmented recordings moulded together into a coherent narrative framework. Beyond the film itself, Blier continued to refute all suggestions that his film aimed at revealing some sort of truth about a whole generation, substantiating the point made above that the film should be regarded primarily and wholly as an endeavour at spectacle

Ils ne constituent pas du tout ... un échantillon représentatif de la jeunesse actuelle. Je n'allais pas jouer à l'enquêteur avec onze bonshommes ... Je les ai choisis parce qu'ils sont photogéniques et parce qu'ils savent parler: deux conditions indispensables à un spectacle. (Garrigou-Lagrange 1963: 13)[3]

2 'What we have here is eleven young people who are, or who will be 20 in 1963. Eleven characters, that's all ... chosen to be in a show, not an enquiry. They may seem to be brought together by the filming, but they never met while the film was being shot.' Note Blier's use of the term *personnages* ('characters') to describe the interviewees, a term which is immediately indicative of a dramatic conception and intention.

3 'They're not meant to be a representative sample of contemporary youth. I wasn't going to pretend to conduct a survey with only eleven guys. I chose them because they are photogenic and articulate: two essential components of any spectacle.'

The film is, then, an exploration of a contradiction: its success depends entirely on the spectator's willingness, and increasingly obligation, to believe in the truth of a visual event he or she knows to be confected. The essential dramatic interest for the spectator lies in the knowledge that the characters on the screen are physi-cally and verbally alienated from each other, and that the conver-sation that develops and gives shape to the film exists only within the diegesis of the filmed sequence: all communication is signalled as being artificial and illusory. Very quickly, the spectator is made aware that authorial and narrative intention are not consistent with the aims of *cinéma-vérité*; Blier's interviews are quite clearly carried out not with the particular aim of ascertaining social truths relating to the lifestyles and opinions of the interviewees, as would be the case in a bona fide *cinéma-vérité* project, but rather in order to highlight the fundamental problem at the heart of the genre: that film is an unreliable means of conveying objective truth.[4]

The technique of direct-to-camera address was developed in a different direction by Blier in some of his major fiction films (most notably *Beau-père, Notre histoire,* and *Trop belle pour toi*), and it has become a key component of the meta-interrogative process of the last three films of his career. *Beau-père* begins with Blier's most sustained direct address to camera, reminiscent in tone of the ironic voice-over of the *film noir*: over the muffled sounds of restaurant activity, Rémi, the pianist, begins to tell his story in a wholly conventional manner and tone

> C'était à l'époque où je travaillais comme pianiste, dans un restaurant panoramique de style cossu international, au premier étage d'un hôtel en forme de tour, avec vue imprenable sur la capitale. Ça aurait pu tout aussi bien se passer à Montréal, à Zurich ou ailleurs. Y aurait eu la même proportion d'Américains, de Japonais, de Saoudiens, les mêmes créatures aux yeux fatigués d'avoir trop compté des dollars. (Blier 1981: 5)[5]

4 For a further discussion of this film, see Harris (1996). On how Blier's recent work is informed by the question of conveying history, see Austin (1994, 73–84).

5 'It was when I was working as a pianist, in a slick international restaurant, on the first floor of a hotel tower, with unbeatable views of Paris. It could easily have been in Montreal, Zurich, or anywhere. There would have been the same number of Americans, Japanese, and Saudis, the same types with strained eyes from too much counting of dollars.'

As the scene develops, we become aware of the fact that the character is speaking over his own music, and as the camera closes in on him, and he begins to fill the frame, so his voice comes to dominate. His gaze follows the camera as it moves around, firmly establishing the viewing spectator as the party to whom the words are spoken. The voice-over here retains the quality of omniscience that we might expect from conventional cinematic usage, but here the comic momentum of the film is that we see, as well as hear, the speaker speak his words, creating a jarring disjunction between the scene before us and the narrative of the film in process. As his voice comments on the extent to which the diners are oblivious to his presence and labour, the action that takes place in the frame, including Rémi's own contribution, is subject to a simultaneous verbal narration by him. First the image dicates the narration with Rémi's 'je pouvais leur jouer n'importe quoi ... de toute façon ils ne m'écoutaient pas' ('I could have played what I liked ... no one ever listened') spoken against a visual and aural background of indifferent diners and their chatter. But as Rémi's narration overtakes the image, a reverse process takes place with verbal narration now determining the image that we and he see. As he says the words 'j'attendais avec impatience ... la fin de la soirée pour aller me coucher' ('I couldn't wait for the end of the night to get to bed'), the camera pans around to a now empty and silent restaurant, providing us with a visual expression of wish fulfilment.

In a similar way, characters in *Trop belle pour toi* often anticipate the next scene with a verbal narration of the events that subsequently take place. In the motel scene, for example, Colette tells herself, the camera and Bernard simultaneously of her desire to 'enregistre bien cette image' ('record this image'), an image which is described by her, and then revealed to us, though not to Bernard who is an integral part of the image. He then describes his 'souvenir' ('memory') of seeing her walk from the shadows, an action which she immediately performs, creating a temporal layering of verbal narration and action, while completing the scene for the spectator, who then sees it in its entirety from an elevated objective view point. In another scene, Pascal narrates the visit of Florence, opening the door in response to the doorbell signalled by his own words, to find her standing there and participating in the unfolding narrative. These 'glissements dans l'intérieur de la scène' ('moments of slippage within the scene' (Audé and Jeancolas 1989: 9)) lend a compelling oneric coherence to the sequences, which problematises the equation 'disruptive technique equals alienation for the spectator'.

However, the link established here between technique and effect is powerfully interrogated by Blier later in the film. After Colette has described how Bernard will leave her and this has been demonstrated, there is a shot of Pascal sitting by the phone, expressing his conviction that 'elle va téléphoner, je sens qu'elle va téléphoner' ('she's going to call. I can feel it. She's going to call'). We cut to a shot of Colette, fully expecting her telephone call to be the next event in the sequence, only to be disappointed in our expectation: not only does Colette not call Pascal, but he has no significant presence in the film after this scene. Thus, the process by which audiences become comfortable with cinematic techniques – even disruptive ones – is explored by Blier within the context of a very practical analysis of the nature of illusion.

Notre histoire makes extensive use of a similar process of dramatic auto-commentary, which is already anticipated in the ironic title of the film. Donatienne, in her second of three incarnations in the film, recounts a scene from 'their' story, and as she does, it is played out for us as an event by the characters themselves. Donatienne takes on the role she now narrates, refusing in turn the new role she has just adopted. The dramatic freedom upon which this technique depends is directly related to the spectator's complicity in the illusion, and his or her willingness to accept the fluidity or flexibility of character implicit in this technique. As Blier himself has stated, 'dans *Notre histoire* ... ce qui m'intéressait, c'était d'amener le public à se poser des questions sur le mécanisme même d'une histoire au cinéma' (Alion 1986, 49).[6] This technique of un-fixed roles, or roles that can change in the course of a production, deliberately refusing the

6 'What interested me in *Notre histoire* was to get spectators to ask themselves questions about how stories are told in film.'

constancy of character common to all literary drama, was of course explored by the *Théâtre du soleil* in many of their major plays.[7] It was equally a feature of the *café-théâtre* style, in which the donning of a suggestion of costume was enough to show that an actor had adopted a different, temporary part. Other examples of the exploration of this technique in Blier's films can be found in *Trop belle pour toi*, where Colette and Florence's lives become interchangeable: although each remains quite visibly in character, there is nevertheless a dramatic reversal of roles where Florence becomes the dowdy drudge waiting for her lover to call, while Colette, *belle* by comparison, dines with her 'husband', and entertains Florence in her home. Blier's experiments with fluidity of characterisation are an intrinsic part of his later films: in *Merci la vie* characters are seen to assume more than one persona, resulting in a complex narrative layering which is left unresolved in the final scene; and in *Un deux trois soleil* the narrative development is marked by the interchangeability of the actions and roles of the majority of characters.

In *Tenue de soirée*, the reference in the final sequence to the existence of Antoine's child constitutes a distortion of even the logic of illogicality that has prevailed in this film, and sees the characterisation and the action lapse into a quasi-fantastic mode. Antoine demonstrates total commitment to the role being performed within the diegesis, which, as it is not real or convincing for the viewer on any level, calls attention to itself as spectacle; the wink to the camera during the credit sequence, confirms this for the viewer. This stylistic self-consciousness is characteristic of Blier's approach, and of the attempt to create a sense of disorder on a wider scale than simply that of characterisation. In *Trop belle*

---

7 For this group, as in for example *1789*, the technique was determined by the imperatives of a huge cast of characters, and the need for mobility in a vast theatrical environment across multiple stages. The scene of the taking of the Bastille involved all actors in direct communication with small groups of spectators, creating the effect of the masses about to revolt. In this relatively new concept for modern theatre audiences, the *Théâtre du soleil* drew their inspiration from traditional popular dramatic forms which tended towards improvisation, and the flexibility of character permitted by this. For a discussion of this scene, see Nes Kirby (1971: 74).

pour toi, for example, the final accusatory direct address to the camera undermines the melodramatic tone of psychological realism (internalised monologue, focus on characters' thoughts and moods) that sometimes appears to dominate in the film. The final accusation equally suggests that this has been a performance, carried out, it would appear, for the spectator's benefit. The devices of filmic narration, most notably located in the fluidity of the camera, and in the decision to film through layers of glass and through partitions, work to make the viewer intensely aware of the emotional consciousness of the central characters, but the final meta-diegetic gesture of the film undermines this, and reminds us forcefully that this is illusory: there is no depth whatsoever to their experience.

The commentary, or mediated narration of the type described above, is a fundamental part of Brechtian theatre, facilitating the dramatic effect that Richard Demarcy has termed '*découpage en tableaux*' ('a breaking into parts'), a formal element of Brechtian Epic theatre in which each scene is self-contained, and prevents an overly empathetic participation in the evolving story on the part of the spectator (Demarcy 1973, 251). In Brecht's view, it is fundamental to a constructive alienation of the audience that: 'the individual episodes have to be knotted together in such a way that the knots are easily noticed ... The parts of the story have to be carefully set off against one another by giving each its own structure as a play within the play' (Willett 1990: 201). The application of this technique within linear and non-linear narrative structures gives many of Blier's scenes their characteristic quality of self-contained, free-standing elements, of '*petite pièce autonome dans la pièce*' ('free-standing sketches within the play' (Demarcy 1973: 251; the italics are Demarcy's)), characterised by digression, interruption and fluidity, and which function independently of linear causality.

The processes of commentary and mediated narration outlined above are complemented elsewhere in Blier's work through the device of the 'integrated spectator', the observer who is a concretised extension of the viewer. In *Notre histoire*, for example, storytelling (to a third party) is encoded in the film title, announcing to the spectator, from the outset, that this is a narrative whose self-conscious aim is to construct a story, to impart a perspective on a relationship. Thus the necessity of a spectator, as the one who receives this story and plays an active part in the process of construction, is immediately established, and the action of spectatorial involvement is itself subsequently enacted within the film. Events are self-consciously acted out or recounted in front of a diegetic audience, and explanations about what is happening are given by central characters to the neighbours who come to see what is going on.

This emphasis on the public event can be traced to Blier's interest in the dramatic potential of group action. The presence of the 'other' on the screen within duos and trios leads inevitably in his work to an explicit use of crowds who observe and form opinions on the unfolding action. These highly stylised crowds, most apparent in the films *Notre histoire, Trop belle pour toi, Merci la vie, Un deux trois soleil* and *Mon homme*, but also present in Blier's earlier work, who sit back and observe the action, often without comment or indeed reaction, function as a theoretical concept, detached from the central performance of the drama, yet wholly integrated into the spectacle. We share with them a perspective on the same action, and to some extent these overtly dramatic crowds concretise the sense of voyeurism, which frequently disturbs spectators. In the later films, the crowd is incorporated ever more forcefully, as real spectators are increasingly distanced from the filmic action and events. Towards the end of *Mon homme* for example, the crowd against which both Marie and Jeannot walk, stops the characters, and offers a series of comments on their actions. In a different vein, strangers, such as the passer-by in the opening scene of *Préparez vos mouchoirs*, witness an essentially private drama unfold, creating a parallel of our own experience as spectators.

The 'other' – whether character or spectator – is a constant and crucial presence in Blier's films, and the key to understanding the logic of the *mise-en-scène*. In *Trop belle pour toi* the conventionally implied internal monologue is verbally exteriorised, with the effect that the characters often appear to speak from within a

dream world, isolated from each other, but privileging the spectator with an expression of their inner emotions. A further conventionally unspoken dimension, that of the expression of sexual
fantasy, is also exteriorised, and this is done via an uninhibited,
and in this case salacious, investment in the language of private
sexual desire: no one reacts to one guest's shocking appreciation
of his hostess Florence as 'quelle salope, quelle merveilleuse
salope' ('what a tart, what a fantastic tart'), thereby implying
complicity, and also hypocrisy of manners in this social milieu.
The distance between what we see – a bourgeois dinner party with
a beautiful hostess – and what we hear – a crude expression of
sexual desire – creates a dramatic tension which disrupts the
spectator's, but crucially not the characters' engagement, with the
illusion of the event. Spectatorial disengagement is maintained by
this, as it is by the pervasive ironic attack on the bourgeois convention of deliberate artificiality in social presentation – behaviour
that might be considered as formally theatrical – and convention:
the wedding speech, for example, is applauded despite its incongruous content. The estrangement of the spectator from the
language, or from the delivery of the language, is heightened by
the placing of the camera *au deuxième degré*, one step removed
from the dramatic action, most frequently in another room,
behind windows and glass partitions. This creates a dual effect of
simultaneous distance and voyeuristic intimacy, encouraging
spectatorial observation rather than involvement.

The self-consciousness of form that is created by the devices
described above is taken a stage further in Blier's work by the
explicit references that are frequently·made to the presence and
function of the component parts of the cinematic image. In *Trop
belle pour toi* and *Merci la vie*, for example, the music on the
soundtrack is alternately as captivating for the characters as it is
for the spectator, or an intrusive presence to which our attention is
drawn by the characters themselves. *Trop belle pour toi* ends with
the accusatory attack by Bernard, 'fait chier votre Schubert' ('your
Schubert makes me sick'), spoken directly to the camera; *Merci la
vie* makes direct reference to the presence of synthesisers on the
soundtrack, and sees the characters comment quite explicitly on

other aspects of the narrative process: Victorine's 'tu sens l'histoire qui s'accélère?' ('can you feel the story gathering pace?') and Camille's 'C'est ça qui s'appelle un flashback?' ('is that what's known as a flashback?') are two examples of the use of this technique. This action of the characters questioning the presence of what is conventionally non-diegetic, is unfamiliar to the spectator, and has the effect of relaunching or reasserting the process of critical viewing: it troubles our emotional investment in the 'story' while amusing us with its intelligent audacity. It is not always as clear as this, however: in *Trop belle pour toi* the spectator, like Bernard, is unable to differentiate at times between the motivated music that results from character action and the non-diegetic soundtrack inserted by the director, making the music an even more powerful component of the absurd dramatic environment of the films.

In all this, Blier crucially problematises the role of the cinematic spectator, the one who watches the drama of the film unfold, but is necessarily alienated from that; he refuses to let the spectator forget that he or she is an intrinsic component of the process of representation, one who must be proactive in their reading of the film. And yet, we are never allowed to forget either that we are on the outside of that process, that our position is one of exteriority and isolation. As well as respecting a Brechtian perspective, this also takes up, from Beckett and absurdist drama, the theme of alienation as the condition of the modern individual.

Characterisation

Blier's work typically displays patterns of characterisation which are consistent and coherent across the corpus. These can be identified as being constructed along three principal axes: first, that of one-dimensionality or types, a construction which, as Richard Dyer has indicated, is unusual for central characters, especially those played by recognisable major stars (Dyer 1981: 246); second, as incarnations of disorder or distortion, displaying grotesque qualities; third, in terms of what might be called cultural collision, and of an unambiguously popular social identity, a pattern which is intensified in aspects of *mise-en-scène* such as setting and material environment, and in the language of the dialogue. The three types of construction, which recall key aspects of absurdist characterisation, are fundamental to the development of a dominant comic tone in Blier's work.

In the comic films, characterisation generally tends towards being schematic or one-dimensional, with characters functioning largely as representatives of certain dramatic or social types. The comic hooligans of *Les Valseuses*, the criminalised misfits of *Buffet froid*, the weak heterosexual and the macho homosexual of *Tenue de soirée*, all function as devices to explore particular character traits, and their inherent ambiguities. The traits of individual characters, peripheral as well as central, are frequently exaggerated to the point of caricature, a device which is used to considerable effect in films as diverse as *Trop belle pour toi* (Florence's beauty) and *Préparez vos mouchoirs* (Solange's passivity). Characteristically, there are defined parameters to roles, with the essential of character behaviour consistent with spectatorial expectations: in *Notre histoire*, the characters identify themselves as *l'ivrogne* (the drunk) and *la nymphomane* (the nymphomaniac); in *Buffet froid*, few characters have names, and they are identified by themselves, and to each other as *l'assassin* (the murderer), *le quidam* (the bloke), *l'inspecteur de police* (the inspector) and *la veuve* (the widow). Rémi in *Beau-père* refers to himself as *le pianiste* (the piano player), bringing a self-conscious commentary to the action, and there are recurrent examples of references to self in the third person in *Trop belle pour toi*, *Merci la vie*, *Un deux trois soleil* and *Mon homme*. The actual names of the characters are of secondary importance, as what they do in the films counts for more than who they are as individuals. Alphonse Tram's role as a type, a dramatic vehicle, rather than a fully drawn psychologically deep individual is, for example, signalled from the outset in the way in which he retains his overcoat at all times.

The assigning of roles in this way is at odds with realist conventions, but is common to the popular theatrical traditions with which Blier's dramatic style engages. The *commedia dell'arte*, for example, from which much modern popular drama has drawn inspiration, dealt largely in fixed or recurrent characterisation, and the dramatic techniques of this form of expression, with its self-consciously theatrical improvisational style involving *personnages fixes, jeu masqué*, a privileging of the grotesque and scatological humour, were a principal influence on the type of theatre produced in *création collective*.[8] The *café-théâtre*'s parodic style depended greatly on the exploration of stereotype and popular expectation about the behaviour of stereotypes, characteristics which are shared by other informal dramatic modes such as circus and music-hall.

The construction of character as incarnation of disorder is a fundamentally distinctive feature of Blier's work, and one that will be explored more fully in the context of carnivalesque expression in the next chapter. For the moment, it is interesting to consider the way in which this characteristic disorder is achieved and expressed through an intense physicality in performance, and through kinesics, or the expressive use of the body in gesture.[9] Characteristically in Blier's films there is an intense focus on the physical dimension of the characters' bodies, and this has been a consistent feature of his work since the early films. Ginette Vincendeau, in her article '*Gérard Depardieu: the Axiom of Contemporary French Cinema*', has discussed the importance of the physical performance of the star to the construction of a consistent dramatic image throughout his career (Vincendeau 1993); this distinctive performance style was first established in the public view in Blier's *Les Valseuses* and developed in the series *Préparez vos mouchoirs, Buffet froid* and *Tenue de soirée*.

The importance of the physical dimension of performance is forcefully apparent from the opening scenes of *Les Valseuses*.

---

8 A full discussion of this is provided in Kourilsky and Champagne (1975: 50 1). Jacques Copeau was also greatly interested in this genre and in its application in modern theatrical performance. See also Jacques Copeau, 'A Theatre of National Renewal' in *Popular Theatre in France* in Campos (1976: 36–7).

9 Esslin defines kinesics as 'the expressive use of the body in gesture' (Esslin 1991: 67). Danny Saunders in O'Sullivan *et al.* (1994: 159) defines it as 'The study of movement and gesture ... associated with the study of the visual mode that is especially involved with body motion and non-verbal communication'.

Vincendeau's analysis of Depardieu's performance concentrates on such physical aspects as 'the aggressive and yet agile display of his massive thickset body': his swagger, tough face, belligerent jutting chin, irregular nose, his insolent tone of voice, and the '1970s sartorial signs of male youth dissent: long hair, flared trousers and a leather jacket'. She sums this up as follows: 'his body and performance provide the "evidence" of heterosexual virility (implied in the social image of the *loubard*) against narrative attempts to undermine it' (Vincendeau 1993: 346–9). Elsewhere in his film-making, Blier has similarly privileged the corporeal qualities of his actors, and the ability to engage with the narrative on a physical level appears to be a consistent and defining criterion of his selection of actors. Of Miou-Miou, for example, he has stated

> C'est une actrice qui a une chose rare: elle a la même violence que Depardieu. Elle peut jouer avec une impudeur qu'elle est seule au monde à avoir. Miou-Miou a avec son corps, avec l'érotisme, une liberté absolue, et en plus elle est drôle et à l'aise, ce qui est sans limites. (Audé and Jeancolas 1989: 10)[10]

Similar qualities have been attributed by Blier to Anouk Grinberg, the star of the final cycle of films

> J'ai eu envie d'écrire pour elle, mais pas comme on écrit normalement un rôle destiné à une fille. J'ai senti qu'elle était comme mon père, capable de jouer comme les hommes, sans aucune des préoccupations qui limitent le rayon d'action des actrices: elle se fiche de son profil, de son physique, de son maquillage. Elle est complètement libre, et c'est très bien. (Riou 1993: 60)[11]

This is signalled from the opening scenes of the three films featuring Grinberg: in *Merci la vie*, Joëlle is initially seen as a victim of

---

10 'There's something unique about her acting ability: she expresses the same violence as Depardieu. She's the only actress who can perform in such an immodest way. Miou-Miou's body and eroticism give her an incredible freedom, as well as which she's funny, she's uninhibited; her range is limitless.'

11 'I wanted to write for her, but not like you normally write for a girl. I felt that she was like my father, capable of performing like a man, without all the concerns that hold actresses back: she doesn't care about the shape of her face, her body, what her make-up is like. She's completely relaxed, and that's just great.'

male aggression, dishevelled in a soiled wedding dress, and is subsequently collected and propelled with little dignity in a shopping trolley by the character who will become her 'buddy'; in *Un deux trois soleil*, the camera focuses in extreme close-up on the magnified face of Victorine, slobbering as she is fed a *tartine*; in *Mon homme*, Marie, the prostitute, poses immobile at the end of an empty arcade, touting her body like any of the other products for sale in the surrounding shop windows. In all three cases, the opening scenes set in motion a series of narrative moments with an increasingly intense, and frequently uncomfortable physical focus.

Blier's conveyance of what might be termed a 'grotesque' quality in characterisation is, in this way, very powerfully achieved; through their physical qualities, the characters are presented as emotionally intense, as visually incongruous and as threatening to any kind of moral or social status quo. The characters, by their presence and actions, are often explicitly disturbing to other characters in the film, and are presented to the spectator in a manner that is frequently visually oppressive, and that defies spectatorial identification. This effect is intensified in Blier's use of multiple characters, especially trios and same-sex duos of characters, as these constitute inherently destabilising units, both sexually and socially.[12] A sense of exclusion is suggested by these repeated dramatic configurations, and by moments of overt conflict between opposing social groupings (criminals–bourgeois, young males–old males etc.). These sub-groups become the intimate focus of films like *Les Valseuses*, *Préparez vos mouchoirs*, *Buffet froid* and *Tenue de soirée*, where the principal characters are featured in almost every scene.

Blier's problematising of the elements of stereotype, typically by presenting characters who have unexpected or apparently incongruous characteristics, is an extensive and structuring element of his work. In her discussion of *Les Valseuses*, Jill Forbes makes it clear that the traits of masculinity and femininity of the two principal male characters are at odds with the expectations

12 Kristin Ross describes the heterosexual couple as the 'new unit of middle class consumption' in the post-war period (Ross 1996: 11).

signalled to the viewer by their physical presence. As Forbes has pointed out

> Depardieu's height, heavy face and more recently, weight seem to predestine him to heavily-coded masculine roles of the kind Belmondo traditionally plays, but Blier also detected in Depardieu a febrility, a sensuality and a vulnerability which apparently contradict or undermine his strongly masculine appearance. Conversely, Dewaere is fragile-looking and slightly effeminate but turns out in the film to be aggressively heterosexual. (Forbes 1992: 177–8)

This cross-typing is carried on across the corpus of Blier's work, and is used to more than simply comic effect. In *Tenue de soirée*, the hulking Bob is the instigator of the homosexual seduction around which the narrative of the film revolves, and, in spite of a forcefully represented overbearing physical male presence, he is a more willing transvestite than Antoine, the character played by Michel Blanc, who achieves a surprising and unsettling femininity in that role. Antoine is slightly built, appears less physically threatening and more sensitive than Bob, but he is more generally aggressive verbally, and more aggressively heterosexual. The same paradox operates in *Merci la vie*, where Joëlle, the conventionally beautiful leading lady who is first seen in the film in a bridal dress, is invested with qualities of verbal coarseness, vulgarity, violence and disease, while, Camille, the plain, unattractive second lead is more wistful, innocent, unworldly and sensitive than her companion. As in much of the Theatre of the Absurd, in Blier's films, this portrayal of character is such that the spectator reacts to them with contradictory feelings, moving between sympathy and revulsion, engagement and distance, remaining at all times in a state of relative incomprehension as to their essential or central nature.

The contradictions within characters create an effective dramatic layering which can be read in terms of patterns of 'cultural collision' which extend to the language and *mise-en-scène* of elements other than those relating directly to character. Blier in fact intensifies the power of the image by using physical types in a way designed to be striking in the frame, and this often depends on patterns of opposition or inversion; the essential dramatic

features of body, gesture and speech to which we would conventionally look for dramatic coherence, are all often at odds with
each other. Characters are typically cast against type, with outward
appearance at odds with character personality, in a way that
problematises the filmic mechanisms of communication and
narrative development. As Forbes points out of Marie-Ange, the
character played by Miou-Miou in *Les Valseuses*, she is 'in
appearance an uninhibited girl, complete with mini-skirt and
contraceptives, yet she takes no pleasure whatsoever in sex and is
not remotely preoccupied with her appearance' (Forbes 1992:
178). Again, in *Tenue de soirée* the huge physical bulk of Bob is at
odds with the gentle physical elegance and verbal and emotional
tenderness that he expresses at points in the film; Antoine's lack
of classic good looks and relative physical insignificance are
equally at odds with the intense desire for him expressed by Bob;
the tenderness of Bob in the love scenes, is coupled with an
inescapable exterior view of him as a stereotyped aggressive, self-
assured, frequently brutish male presence. Thus, the depth and
apparent sincerity of his potentially camp declaration, 'je ferai de
toi une reine' ('I'll turn you into a queen'), are all the more
powerful given this unavoidable and constant reminder that he
seems outwardly to be incapable of such depths of emotion. Blier's
tendency towards caricature rejects safe stereotypes in favour of
an interrogation of social interaction, social trends and group
behaviour. In Blier's work this is all the more interesting for
taking place within the framework and traditions of farce and
burlesque comedy, which more commonly reinforce simple
notions of stereotype.

In more general dramatic terms, the recurrence of duos of
characters, particularly males, in interdependent relationships
recalls the work of all the major absurdists, from Beckett's many
tragi-comic pairings (Vladimir–Estragon, Hamm–Clov, Winnie–
Willie) to Ionesco's Smiths, and *'les vieux'* to Genet's *'les bonnes'*.[13]
Les Valseuses, *Préparez vos mouchoirs*, *Buffet froid* and *Tenue de*

---

13 The plays referred to here are: Samuel Beckett's *En attendant Godot*, *Fin de partie*
and *Oh les beaux jours*; Eugène Ionesco's *La Cantatrice chauve* and *Les Chaises*;
and Jean Genet's *Les Bonnes*.

soirée all demonstrate stylised dramatic routines involving two or three characters, and the nature of the synchronisation is such that there is frequently a sense of movement around a stage space. The opening scene of *Buffet froid*, for example, is composed of seven minutes of intense stichomythic dialogue, with movement restricted to a rhythmic circling of a fixed arrangement of seats. The dimensions of the dramatic environment are large (the *la Défense* RER station), but movement is restricted to a small central area, intensified by the symmetrical nature of the material environment. Interaction between the characters is the main dynamic of the narrative of all Blier's films, and this effect is intensified by the casting of a permutation of actors across films. Blier's stylistic preferences for speech-based, relatively static scenes, exploring either situations rather than actions, or actions within situations, forcefully recall the exercises in 'killing time' that constitute the central dynamic of Beckett's *En attendant Godot*. The central Mozart scene in *Préparez vos mouchoirs* is an example of this technique: the characters simply sit and voice a fantasy about the appearance of Mozart, an action that in no way advances the resolution of the narrative dilemma, but passes the time.[14] Again, in the riverside fishing scene in *Les Valseuses*, the series of clichés articulated by the characters – 'j'adore la première cigarette de la journée; ça remet la bouche en forme' ('I love the first cigarette of the day; it wakes your mouth up') – functions as dialogue of exchange rather than advancement. This is all the more effective for being set against the background of the classic inactivity of men fishing.

The recurrent themes of criminality and deviant sexuality, the attention given to the character of the *voyou flamboyant* (the flamboyant lout) and the location of much of the dramatic action in what Blier himself terms an 'univers carcéral' ('carceral universe' (Michaux 1986: 60)) all point to a further absurdist influence in Blier's work, that of the novelist and dramatist Jean

---

14 Blier claims that this scene was in fact his inspiration for the film: 'D'autres fois, je pars d'une scène. *Préparez vos mouchoirs* a été écrit par le milieu: c'est parti d'une scène sur Mozart' ('other times I start from a single scene. *Préparez vos mouchoirs* was written from the middle, from the Mozart scene' (Chevrie and Dubroux 1985: 12)).

Genet. At the time of the release of *Tenue de soirée*, in which admittedly the parallels are immediately striking, Blier responded to the question 'Avez-vous pensé à Genet, au "Journal du voleur"? ... les voyous, les taulards semblent vous fasciner' as follows: 'J'avais emporté les bouquins de Genet sur le tournage. Je ne les ai pas ouverts, mais ils étaient là ...'.[15] Blier's work ressembles Genet's on a number of levels, appearing to draw directly on particular aspects of his dramatic conception, most notably the exploration of a generalised deviant sexuality or sexual appetite, the ritualistic aspects of performance (repetition of actions and situations) and the inscription of theatricality within performance (adoption of roles and costume in particular).

The main characters of the majority of Blier's films epitomise the same qualities of marginality and exclusion as Beckett's, the same transgressive impulses as those of Genet, and the same lack of direction as Ionesco's. As such, these characters embody a social image which is fundamentally menacing to observers, diegetic and non-diegetic. Yet, like Beckett's figures, Blier's heroes, 'des héros qui sont généralement des pauvres types, des cloches, des paumés' ('heroes who are poor souls, fools, misfits' (Haustrate 1988: 109)) embody tragic qualities which find their most poignant expression in an accessible urban and social context. The characters generally, especially as incarnated by Depardieu, Dewaere, Blanc, Miou-Miou and Balasko, are all distinctly plebeian in their social construction, and this is the quality that Blier privileges in his choice of actors and in his narratives. The main characters of the majority of the films, in the absence of evident employment or labour, are defined most immediately and fully by the actions that focus their energies: these actions tend to be either leisure-oriented and therefore overtly challenging to the dominant production–consumer ideology (in *Les Valseuses* this takes the form of the repeated theft of cars, the iconic consumer good of the post-war period) or they demonstrate an explicit desire for physical gratification above all else. In both cases, the films share a

15 'Were you thinking of Genet, of his *Journal du Voleur*? ... yobs, old lags, you seem fascinated by them'. Blier: 'I had taken Genet's works on set with me. I didn't actually open them, but they were there ...' (Michaux 1986: 60).

clear sense of these characters being excluded from wider society where pleasure and leisure are secondary to the impulses towards production and self-restraint.

The stylisation of space: *Buffet froid* (1979)

A dynamic stylisation of the dramatic environment, which enhances, develops and extends the thematic and active absurdity of the films, is a further important element of the overall conception in Blier's films. *Buffet froid* is the most striking and arguably successful example of how the thematic anxieties of surveillance/observation, social exclusion and absurd illogicality are projected onto the dramatic environment.

The film begins, as it proceeds, with the defamiliarising of an unambiguously familiar setting: the dazzling, intensely angular, mechanical environment of the deserted *La Défense* RER station, naturalistic in its functionality and banality, but stylised in its selective representation by the camera. By emptying it of all elements other than the two principal characters, and by focusing on the symmetrical aspects of the material features, Blier creates a scene – and a film – that is highly stylised in its spatial aspect. The figure of Alphonse Tram (Gérard Depardieu) intrudes noisily into this ultra-modern and menacing landscape, and engages in a series of actions conducted on the principles of symmetry and counterbalance reflected in the surrounding material environment. The scene is artificially lit, supplementary props (such as the knife) are rare and take on a heightened, intrusive aspect, physical action is kept to a minimum, and the takes are long and predominantly static. A motif of avoidance and pursuit, central to the subsequent narrative development, is established in this scene as Tram endeavours to engage a wary stranger in a conversation, whose random nature and seemingly absurd speculations remind the viewer of Samuel Beckett's exercises in 'passing the time'. As the *quidam* ('bloke' played by Michel Serrault) finds himself increasingly ensnared in Tram's compelling appeals for social exchange, we see the two men sitting together in medium shot in similar dress – heavy overcoats, in identical poses – hands clasped in front of them. The comic potential of the dramatic situation is suddenly expoited in a way that defuses the pervasive sense of alienation and estrangement that has dominated so far, of which the environment is an integral part.

The dramatic framework of this opening sequence anticipates the axes along which the subsequent action of the film develops. *Buffet froid* remains characterised by long takes on relatively static action, by a centralising of the protagonists within a series of frames, either of the camera itself or located within the horizontal and vertical axes of the diegetic environment (doors, corridors, lifts, packing cases, even the spiral staircase), a technique that Blier later refined in *Trop belle pour toi*. The angularity of the material environment, coupled with the general use of weak spots of light, has a highly stylising effect reminiscent of *film noir*, highlighting relative position and giving depth to the physical relations of the frequently static subjects. Movement such as it is in this film is measured, but fluid, almost ritualistic in the way in which the banal, everyday actions of opening and closing doors, sitting at the table, or walking within expansive spaces is highlighted. This visual centring of minimal action inevitably compels the viewer to concentrate on the verbal dynamism of the dialogue. The rapid verbal repartee acts as a complement to both the static performance style and the restricted view that the spectator – and protagonists – have of the action. The dialogic nature of the exchange – comic in its frequent incongruity, but also confrontational, conflictual – enhances the sinister setting and atmosphere of the film in which the words themselves seem to conjure up realities on the model of the worst possible nightmare. In *Buffet froid*, the next thing to happen always develops from the events of the previous scene, but functions on a paradoxical principle of opposition: it is always a confirmation of the fears already expressed by the characters about exactly what they hope will *not* happen. Tram expresses the fear that he will kill someone in the *métro*, and in the next scene someone lies dying with Tram's knife in his stomach; he imagines that his victim could be passed by – 'on dirait un clochard qui roupille' ('you'd say it was a tramp asleep') leading to the next scene where the stabbed *quidam* is lying in a métro corridor in exactly the same pose as the tramps around him; Tram's wife ridicules his admonition that she should be careful with the words 'est-ce que j'ai une tête à me faire assassiner?' ('do I look like someone who'd get herself killed?'), only to be found murdered in the next scene, and so on, throughout the film. In this way, as each scene announces the next, with the staging of events signalled by a perverse process of auto-commentary, the spectator is constantly reminded of the process of narrative construction underlying the action of the film.

Later in the film, when the action finally takes place in a feeble daylight scene, the three main characters are featured in a semi-circular static position, 'allongés dans des chaises longues devant la maison, à l'ombre, l'inspecteur et l'assassin emmit"ifflés dans des couvertures' ('lying in deck chairs in front of the house, in the shade, the inspector and the murderer wrapped up in blankets' (Blier 1980: 64)). They are dwarfed by the house behind them and by the expanse of nature that surrounds them, an environment which they do not understand, and which they look upon with apprehension and hostility. The many references in this scene to the cold and the damp, to the inspector's painful feet, to the sinister changes in the natural environment (the birds suddenly stop singing), coupled with recriminations and reproaches, and the pleas to 'rester groupés' ('stay together'), 'faut pas se séparer' ('mustn't get separated') when Alphonse proposes to 'faire un tour' ('have a look around'), signal as intertext the exchanges between Vladimir and Estragon in Beckett's *Waiting for Godot*. This is intensified by the fact that most of the conversation takes place between only two characters (Alphonse and l'Inspecteur), who argue, but do not separate from each other, and by the arrival of an unexpected individual, 'l'homme en bleu' ('the man in blue') who in both his formality and unclear intentions recalls Beckett's Pozzo in the same play. What is interesting here is that this scene is filmed in a 'très lent travelling avant qui va durer tout le temps de la conversation entre les trois hommes' ('very slow forward tracking shot which lasts the entire length of the men's conver-sation'), a technique which keeps the characters fixed in relation to each other and to the spatial dimensions of their dramatic environment. The pervasive sense of menace which this *mise-en-scène* conveys is entirely consistent with the nightmarish illogicality of the film's narrative.

Subversion of the atmospheric qualities of the naturalist/realist environment is an extension of Blier's treatment of the spatial environment, and is clearly a technique that he relishes. In all of the films, the environment is to some extent naturalistic, but it is increasingly theatrically defamiliarised in the course of the film: as Blier himself has said 'il n'y a jamais personne dans mes films. On va dans la rue, elle est vide. Le métro est vide. Il y a bien une rame mais personne dedans' ('there's never anyone in my films. Go in the street, it's empty. The underground is empty. There might be a train, but there's no one in it' (Le Guay 1986: 22)). The dramatic architecture of Blier's films is very frequently conveyed through an aesthetic of emptiness and desertification, where the familiar and immediately recognisable are made strikingly unfamiliar. In both *Les Valseuses* and *Préparez vos mouchoirs*, for example, the main characters go to a seaside town out of season. As the normal activity and purpose of a seaside town are ignored, and the function of the environment is reversed, so it is cinematically and narratively defamiliarised, and thereby rendered all the more highly stylised. Again, this is repeated throughout *Buffet froid*, *Préparez vos mouchoirs* and *Tenue de soirée* in the many shots of streets emptied of cars, and of buildings apparently devoid of inhabitants: the process of defamiliarising thus heightens atmosphere, distancing the object or scene viewed from the real, even though what we see could not be photographically more convincing. A variation on this is seen at the end of *Buffet froid*, where Blier constructs a theatrical scene around the hyper-realistic setting of an expansive outdoor scene. Again, there is precise control of the dramatic elements in this *mise-en-scène*, with the principal focus on the use of colour and on economy of action, contrasting movement and stasis in a highly dramatic manner. *Avant-scène 244, Buffet froid* describes the shot sequence of this final scene in terms of a series of dominant wide and long shots, interspersed with close shots of the characters: 'plan général de la rivière, la barque à l'arrière-plan' ('long shot of the river, the boat in the background); 'plan général. La barque au milieu de la rivière, coulant dans les gorges de plus en plus encaissées, dans lesquelles le soleil ne pénètre plus' ('long shot. Boat in the middle of the river, going towards steep gorges, where the sun no longer reaches); 'Plan large: la barque toute petite au milieu du décor écrasant; nouveau plan large, encore plus large que le précédent, avec la barque minuscule et les personnages à peine visibles tout au fond de l'image' ('long shot; tiny boat in the middle of an overwhelming décor; further long shot, even longer than the last one; minute boat with the occupants barely visible at the back of the frame'); 'Cadrage sur un coude de la rivière. La nuit est presque tombée. Musique. La barque glisse sur l'eau. Puis elle disparaît du champ' ('Framing of a bend in the river. Almost complete darkness. The boat slides on the water. Then it disappears out of shot' (Blier 1980: 70–1)). Here, it is the unusually intense focus, at the moment of narrative conclusion, on the structural elements of the environment rather than those of character action and interaction, which reinforces the atmosphere of alienation and desperation so central to the thematic base of the film.

The notion of a dynamic dramatic environment is taken up again in *Trop belle pour toi*, where the alienation of the characters, from each other and from the spectator, is dramatically encoded in the spatial dimension of the film. The absence of patterns of cause and effect, which might explain the romantic situation to the spectator, results in the spectator focusing more intensely on the dramatic environment. However, the images in this work, filmed from behind glass partitions and through the labyrinthine glass corridors of Bernard's office, serve to intensify the sense of distance and of spectatorial impotence: the spectator's inability to become involved is thus in many ways mocked by the dramatic environment. What Blier manages to achieve here is 'la liberté d'action par rapport à l'espace, et la liberté du point de vue par rapport à l'action' through the deliberate creation of 'une certaine artificialité, une transposition poussée du décor théâtral' (Bazin 1994: 139).[16]

16 'Freedom of action in relation to space, and freedom of point of view in relation to action' through 'a certain artificiality, a forced transposition of the material dramatic environment'.

Blier's films subvert the narrative coherence of classic narrative cinema through a modification of the classic dramatic unities of time, space and action. This disruption is not simply about a nihilistic negation of forms, but is clearly formulated in relation to an understanding of, and respect for, established and very familiar conventions of *mise-en-scène* and narrative action – not, perhaps, within cinema, but certainly within French theatrical traditions. What is particularly innovative about Blier's cinema is, then, his engagement with past dramatic forms, particularly those that embody an informed use of 'artistic collisions'. As we have seen, the absurd incoherence that characterises Blier's work is in fact, very coherent indeed.

References

Alion, Yves (1986), 'Entretien avec Bertrand Blier', *Revue du cinéma* 417, June.

Audé, Françoise and Jeancolas, Jean-Pierre (1989), 'Entretien avec Bertrand Blier', *Positif*, May.

Austin, Guy (1994), 'History and Spectacle in Blier's *Merci la vie*', *French Cultural Studies* 5, 73–84.

Bazin, André (1994), *Qu'est-ce que le cinéma?*, Paris, Éditions du Cerf.

Blier, Bertrand (1980), *Buffet froid*, Avant-scène du Cinéma 244, 15 March.

Bradby, David (1991), *Modern French Drama 1940–1990* (2nd edn), Cambridge, Cambridge University Press.

Chevrie, Marc and Dubroux, Danièle (1985), 'A la recherche de l'histoire: entretien avec Bertrand Blier', *Cahiers du cinéma* 371–2, May, 12.

Campos, Christophe (1976), *Theatre Quarterly* 6:23, autumn 36–7.

Demarcy, Richard (1973), *Éléments d'une sociologie du spectacle*, Paris, UGE.

Dyer, Richard (1981), 'The Stars as Signs', in Bennett, Boyd-Bowman *et al.* (eds), *Popular Television and Film*, London, BFI/OU, 246.

Esslin, Martin (1972), *The Theatre of the Absurd* (revised edn), London, Pelican.

Esslin, Marin (1991), *The Field of Drama: How the Signs of Drama Create Meaning on Stage and Screen*, London, Methuen.

Forbes, Jill (1992), *The Cinema in France: After the New Wave*, London, Macmillan.

Garrigou-Lagrange, Madeleine (1963), 'Hitler, connais pas', *Témoignage Chrétien* 8 August, 13.

Harris, Sue (1996), '*Hitler, connais pas!* Bertrand Blier's Apprenticeship in the Techniques of Spectacle', *French Cultural Studies* 7, 295–307.

Haustrate, Gaston (1988), *Bertrand Blier*, Paris, Edilig.

Hayward, Susan (1996), *Key Concepts in Cinema Studies*, London, Routledge.

Kourilsky and Champagne (1975), 'Political Theatre in France since 1968', *The Drama Review* (Political Theatre Issue) 19:2, June.

Le Guay, Philippe (1986), 'Entretien avec Bertrand Blier', *Cinématographe* 119, May.

Michaux, Sylvie (1986), 'Bertrand Blier: Une fantastique admiration pour la femme ...' *Le Nouvel Observateur* 1119, 18 April, 60.

Nes Kirby, Victoria (1971), *1789*, The Drama Review (European Performance Issue), 15·4, autumn, 74.

O'Sullivan, T., J. Hartley, D. Saunders, M. Montgomery and J. Fiske (1994), *Key Concepts in Communication and Cultural Studies*, London and New York, Routledge.

Riou, Alain (1993), 'L'Impossible Monsieur B.B.', *Nouvel Observateur* 1502, 19 August. 60.

Ross, Kristin (1996), *Fast Cars, Clean Bodies: Decolonization and the Reordering of French Culture*, MIT Press, 11.

Vincendeau, Ginette (1994), 'Gérard Depardieu: the Axiom of Contemporary French Cinema', *Screen*, winter, 343–51.

Willett, John (1990) (ed. and trans.), *Brecht on Theatre: the Development of an Aesthetic* London, Methuen Drama.

3

Festive madness: the carnival as structuring motif[1]

The comic momentum of Blier's films relies on the elaboration of a system of images which might be termed 'festive–ludic' or 'anarcho-comic'. The films are characterised by the creation of a diegetic universe in which normal orders, relations, roles and positions are routinely reversed; rules of social and dramatic logic are inverted, and contradictions in characterisation and in character interaction are commonplace. This aesthetic reordering of the conventional dramatic and cultural codes of character construction, along with the active manipulation of patterns of linearity and psychological realism common to filmic texts, is part of the discourse of subversion that underpins Blier's cinema: what emerges very clearly in Blier's films is the sense of a challenge to the hegemonic rules of filmic expression, especially as they relate to an understanding of popular forms.

These formal inversions draw on specifically carnivalesque festive forms, which translate into a coherent system of images and references and function as structuring motifs across the corpus of films. The comic framework of the carnival is apparent in many surface aspects of the films: the enjoyment of the libertarian and the scatological, the debasement of cultural assumptions, the focus on grotesque bodily symbolism, and attacks on social decorum. A generalised sense of the ludic, signalled in

---

1 An early version of parts of this chapter appeared in Chapter 8: 'The people's film-maker? *Théâtre populaire* and the films of Bertrand Blier' in Perry and Cross (1997).

recurrent displays of verbal and physical contempt for systems of authority, respect and order, dominates in both the dramatic content and narrative structures of the films. This is explored explicitly in the social companionship, active fraternity and sexual consent that is the basis of all the central relationships in the films, and it is echoed in both the predominance of increasingly elliptical and non-linear narrative forms, and in an evolving device of non-stable characterisation. Constraint and limitation, both aesthetic and in terms of visual and verbal content, are increasingly rejected in favour of a festive narrative framework, in which images of bodily life (principally the actions of eating, drinking and sex) are indicative of a privileging by the characters of the instinctive and physical dimensions of being, rather than the rational or scientific. Similarly, images of social gatherings, frequently involving the consumption of food, or unity of action (processions, dramatic synchronisation) further this sense of *fête*. Blier's recurrent thematic concerns with questions of virility, fertility, community, the currency of sexual behaviour and habits, and his parodic ludic focus on the dramatic manifestations of this, are further indicative of a concept of festivity in his treatment of matters of social interaction.

The concept of 'festive madness', where the observer looks at the world through different eyes, 'not dimmed by "normal", that is by commonplace ideas and judgements' (Bakhtin 1984: 39) is central to Mikhail Bakhtin's assessment of the popular carnivalesque tradition, and to a proposed carnivalesque reading of Blier's films. Blier's rejection of an easy identification with the normal and the commonplace is liberating for both protagonists and spectators: as in the traditional carnival, expressions of excess or threats to normal order are channelled into the representation of the sexuality of the characters, and are echoed in other aspects of their character, actions and experiences; in Blier's work this is not feared in any way, but actively celebrated. The characters are engaging as well as menacing, mocked as well as mocking.

For Bakhtin, carnival laughter is festive, universal in scope, 'directed at all and everyone, including the carnival's participants' (Bakhtin 1984: 11) and ambivalent, that is, simultaneously triumphant and deriding, mocking and assertive. It is, for him, the single defining mechanism of folk culture. As he has stated

> For thousands of years folk culture strove at every stage of its development to overcome by laughter, render sober, and express in the language of the material lower bodily stratum (in an ambivalent sense) all the central ideas, images and symbols of official cultures. (Bakhtin 1984: 394)

Robert Stam has taken this point up by noting that

> The culture of real laughter ... is absolutely central to Bakhtin's conception of carnival: enormous, creative, derisive, renewing laughter that grasps phenomena in the process of change and transition, finding in every victory a defeat and in every defeat a potential victory. Laughter for Bakhtin has a cognitive value ... Carnivalesque laughter can be raucous, subversive, even angry, a laughter that erases old differences and installs new, unstable ones. Laughter is profound, communitarian, erotic, a current passing from self to self in a free and familiar atmosphere. (Stam 1992: 119–20)

Blier's carnivalesque assertion of social and aesthetic liberty is indissociable from the period and place of its creation, that is post-1968 France, and is indicative of a politically subversive discourse underlying his work. His most striking and original work, *Les Valseuses*, was produced in what might with justification be termed a post-revolutionary era, and in it Blier acknowledges the dominant political discourse of contestation, while mounting a challenge to the prevailing view of society communicated through the cultural apparatus of the artistically 'acceptable'. Blier's *Les Valseuses* is an early and important example of the new kind of subversive commentary that evolved within this society, seen in *café-théâtre* and the magazine culture of *Pilote* and *Hara-Kiri*, and more generally in the changing habits and lifestyles of the post-1968 generation. Working within an established literary satirical tradition of Rabelaisian observation, Blier's work can be said to embody the same desire to destroy what Bakhtin terms the 'official picture of events' (Bakhtin 1984: 439) by showing a dissenting view of society and the people, and thereby challenging the

prevailing order. Yet, far from displaying an attitude of misanthropy, Blier's is arguably a profoundly democratic view insofar
as it expresses opposition to the official mainstream, conformist,
authoritarian view of the times. Ideologically, then, in terms of his
association with, and exploitation of, the images and structures of
an established popular subversive culture, Blier's work can be
read in the context of modern cultural and political subversion,
with his inspiration lying in the older traditional dramatic forms
of this expression and, by extension, with the contemporary inter-
preters and interpretations of these forms. As such, it is possible
to consider his work as a cinematic expression, and indeed
dramatisation, of the same folk culture of subversive humour
within which Rabelais' work functions, and within which Bakhtin
and later commentators have analysed popular cultural forms.

The grotesque body

The ludic dimension to Blier's work, the intense focus on comic
types and formulas, the tendency towards dramatic hyperbole and
the desire to construct 'a corporeal semiotic cebebrating the
grotesque, excessive body and the "orifices" and "protruberances"
of the "lower bodily stratum"' (Stam 1992: 93), associate him very
clearly with what Bakhtin has termed the 'one culture of folk
carnival humour' (Bakhtin 1984: 4). Mikhail Bakhtin's concept of
grotesque realism as related to the subject of popular carnival is
directly applicable to Blier's exploration of the ludic in film, an
exploration which depends, as does Rabelais' work, on a particularly popular approach to aspects of language, character, parody
and festive action. To use Bakhtin's categories, Blier works not
within the romantic grotesque tradition, that inspires fear, menace
or alienation as might seem the case during the opening scenes of
almost all of his films, particularly *Les Valseuses, Tenue de soirée,*
Buffet froid, and *Merci la vie,* but within a carnivalesque grotesque
tradition where 'all that was frightening in ordinary life is turned
into amusing or ludicrous monstrosities' (Bakhtin 1984: 47).

Blier's characters, particularly those incarnated by Depardieu,

Dewaere and Grinberg across a range of films, are deliberately disconcerting, and somewhat grotesque both in physical and psychological nature. These characters, like the clowns or fools of the carnival, as well as those created by Beckett and Ionesco in the Theatre of the Absurd, have their antecedents in traditions of comic Saturnalia, and their comic persona is constructed in a similar way. They do not set out to be comic, and tend to express incomprehension, rather than a sense of comedy, at the events and actions around them; they observe life and comment on what they see and experience, and the comedy arises from the distance between what they see from the outside, and what we see them to be within the context of their diegetic society. The very careful choreography of the actions of two or more characters in the frame is evidence to the spectator of the strangeness and grotesqueness of these characters, of their difference and distance from their society and environment: they are misfits, theatrical constructs whose movement is not naturalistic, and whose actions are frequently no more than responses triggered by the dramatic events. Yet they are wholly a part of their own society, which has an internal logic and coherence, and in which they play a full part.

An attention to disconcerting or grotesque qualities in character construction generally is common to all Blier's films, and is achieved by a focus on three major dramatic aspects of the body: the build or physical comportement of the individual characters, the body in movement or gesturing, and the body in relation to others, all three factors allowing for a certain choreography of movement for dramatic effect. The narrative and stylistic economy of *Les Valseuses* draws heavily on these features. For example, as the film nears its conclusion, in a scene reminiscent of the circus clowns and their traditional exploding car, the dramatic focus centres on the physical action of the characters in relation to each other: Jean-Claude's verbal outburst and active attempt to deal with the problem with the stolen car's engine are comically contrasted by the positioning and relative inaction of Marie-Ange and Pierrot, who do not budge from their kissing pose in the back of the car. The subsequent scene, in which the three characters attempt to hitch a lift, exemplifies the expressive use of the body in gesture: in a theatrical set piece, the characters' qualities of failure, insolence and daring are intensified in the stylised nature of their gesturing, and in the way in which they sit or lie. The physical type of each character adds to this: the menacing frame of Jean-Claude, the carelessness and lack of inhibition of Marie-Ange, and the comic cheek – facial and physical – of Pierrot are necessarily perceived as a continuum, expressing *ennui* and contempt for their situation. In this scene, the proximity and visual realism of actual cars going past is irrelevant; the essence of the scene is contained in the dramatic mechanisms, and in the dramatic creation of non-naturalistic parody.

The grotesque is also conveyed in a frequently scatological concentration on the bodily functions, and an attenuated Rabelaisian approach to matters of sexual activity, consumption of food and the general physical nature of the body. In his films, Blier dramatically explores cultural and aesthetic taboos which have traditionally been associated with the physical and sexual nature of the human body, and he frequently and controversially does this with regard to specifically female representation. In *Préparez vos mouchoirs*, for example, the focus is on the fertility of the principal female character and the efforts of the males to impregnate her. The desire for sexual consummation is the driving force of *Tenue de soirée*, and *Les Valseuses* concentrates at various points on the physical action of the body related to breast feeding, genital odour, and bathing. Similarly, the sexual activity of the lead female characters in *Merci la Vie* and *Mon homme* is the catalyst for the narrative development. What has problematised the reading of Blier's carnivalesque bodily system of images is, however, that audiences typically bring late twentieth-century systems of analysis and values to them, that inevitably lead to an interpretation of them that takes account of the modern political consciousness. Yet, as Bakhtin's analysis makes clear, preoccupations of this kind with the 'lower bodily stratum' (Bakhtin 1984: 55) are characteristic of folk humour, and can be situated without controversy in the long-established 'concept of grotesque realism' where 'the bodily element is deeply positive' (Bakhtin 1984: 18–19). Blier's focus on expressly sexual subject-matter and his employment of

recurrent images of the sexual nature of his characters can therefore be read as consistent with those of carnival and its characteristic reduction of the spiritual and the abstract to a material
level. In this popular dramatic conception, the intellectual and
creative value of the image of the body, essential to and unproblematic within the carnival tradition, is necessarily privileged, and
the implicit de-eroticising of the nude body is evidence of the functioning of a subversive mechanism within the dramatic construction.

Much of the shock value of these images and expressions is in
fact derived from the public expression of what is usually relegated to an unspoken level, and this is true both within the film
and with respect to the manifestation of this type of expression in
the aesthetically determined medium of cinema. In Blier's work,
however, there is little place for privacy or the private experience,
the functioning of the body hidden away from its social context, as
this necessarily denies the social aspect of the collective experience. What the exposition of the body in this way allows Blier to
develop is the thesis underlying the narrative of *Hitler, connais
pas!*, which acknowledged that cinema, as an expressive medium,
is fundamentally unsuited to recording the private experience:
there is always a spectator, an observer, an outsider who invades
the privacy of the intimate moment. Thus, in an elaboration of the
techniques employed in *Hitler, connais pas!*, Blier's adoption in his
later films of a dramatic grotesque reference functions to explore
the limitations of cinema, and highlights its purpose, consistent
with that of Brechtian theatre, as a vehicle of mediation rather
than of truth.

The carnivalesque grotesque typically shows two contradictory
aspects of life simultaneously. As Bakhtin has suggested

> We find at the basis of grotesque imagery a special concept of the
> body as a whole and of the limits of this whole. The confines
> between the body and the world and between separate bodies are
> drawn in the grotesque genre quite differently than in the classic
> and naturalist images. [...] The grotesque ignores the impenetrable
> surface that closes and limits the body as a separate and completed
> phenomenon ... grotesque imagery constructs what we might call
> a double body. (Bakhtin 1984: 315/318)

This reading of the grotesque as duality, and of grotesque duality as a fundamental concept of the bodily system of images of popular culture, lends a further level of interest to Blier's characteristic use of duos of characters across the body of his work. The traditional symbolic couplings of life–death, youth–age, male–female, all related to the principle of renewal and renascence, are echoed in Blier's films in the recurrent dramatic pairing of characters who are perceived to have opposing, and to some extent mutually exclusive dominant characteristics. The male and the female are contrasted and explored in the male characters of *Les Valseuses*, the flamboyant and the timid in *Tenue de soirée*, law and criminality in *Buffet froid*, the diseased and the pure or innocent in *Merci la vie*, and the beautiful and the plain are explored in the female characters in *Trop belle pour toi*. In this way, Blier's work refuses to engage with what Bakhtin terms 'the new bodily canon' of modern literary forms which

> in all its historic variations and different genres, presents an entirely finished, completed, strictly limited body, which is shown from the outside as something individual ... The basis of the image is the individual, strictly limited mass, the impenetrable façade. (Bakhtin 1984: 320)

Blier's exploration of this popular trope is demonstrated in processes of narrative and dramatic *rapprochement*. In *Les Valseuses*, the two male characters are gradually perceived to grow closer until they seem to be more two parts of one whole, indissociable, than two individual beings. The same organic effect is achieved in *Préparez vos mouchoirs* where, although the male characters are not so obviously different in their construction, they are contrasted first as opposites in their attitude to a given situation, and later as complementary dramatic elements: what emerges in both films is a certain grotesque quality to the comic paralleling of their actions. For example, both the riverside scene in *Les Valseuses*, and the scene of Solange's disappearance in *Préparez vos mouchoirs*, function on principles of parallel actions, identical dress, and verbal complementarity: the extension of the concept of the grotesque body is here extended to a dramatic synchronisation of male behaviour which intensifies the carnivalesque expression of community experience, and removes any sense of an individualised image.

In a further exploration of carnivalesque duality, Blier's grotesque is suggestive of a combination of the animal and the human, one of the most ancient grotesque forms, in which the animal is equated with unrestrained or uncontrolled emotions, instincts and actions (Bakhtin 1984: 316) The secondary characters in Blier's films are evidence of the extension of this concept beyond the patterns of characterisation of the central characters: the man mirrored by his dog at the beginning of *Les Valseuses*, the brutal pimp in *Tenue de soirée* and the predatory doctor in *Merci la vie*, are all constructed in this way. But it is essentially within the actions of the principal characters that we see this element, frequently bound up with a tone of threat or menace implicit in the unleashing of these emotions. Bob in *Tenue de soirée* illustrates this point: from the outset he is represented as a wild character, someone whose excessive behaviour and imagination disturb the status quo. He is transgressive on a number of levels: he is a criminal who has been imprisoned, he is bisexual, he has unexplained access to large amounts of money, has no obvious abode, and throughout the film, he is physically dominant over the small, slight figures of Antoine and Monique. His menacing stance, established in the opening scene, is maintained until the end of the film, when the nature of the menace becomes defused in an excess of comic imagination. Yet he is equally a tender, engaging seducer and a compelling screen presence for the spectator, and this unambiguous exposition of the mechanisms of duality therefore functions in a self-conscious and wholly carnivalesque manner.

Images of physical grotesqueness are an established and recurrent feature of popular imagery from *images d'Epinal* to *bande dessinée*, through the comic films of Chaplin, Tati *et al.*, and in *Rabelais and his world*, Bakhtin documents the revival of the grotesque in modern French theatrical forms, especially in those explored by Jarry and Brecht (Bakhtin 1984: 46). Blier's dramatic exploration of such a concept therefore recalls a specifically popular iconographic system of reference, and a particularly modern theatrical frame of reference. This type of theatrical approach is close to Brecht's theories of epic theatre, which display a similar requirement to strip away all that is naturalistic, as well as to that of *café-théâtre*, which deals largely in dramatic hyperbole and patterns of parodic distortion.

The transgressive impulse

Blier's films are populated by transgressive characters, who tend to be defined in terms of a self-imposed marginality, most often translated into acts of criminality and general social deviance, and they are all the more transgressive in their apparent hedonistic enjoyment of this state. The principal characters of the later films in particular have tended to be explicitly deviant characters, whose presence and actions pose a threat to the outwardly stable society of which they are a part. Figures such as the 'pute par vocation' (*Mon homme*), the negligent mother and alcoholic father (*Un deux trois soleil*), the promiscuous diseased woman (*Merci la vie*), the errant husband (*Trop belle pour toi*), the criminal homosexual (*Tenue de soirée*), and the murderers and corrupt police inspector (*Buffet froid*) are forcefully destabilising constructs, whose behaviour and patterns of motivation in the films complicate the process of spectatorial interpretation. The refusal by the director to cast these characters in terms of conventional patterns of central character evolution – transgression followed by awareness of the error and eventual redemption (Hayward 1996: 251) – compounds this difficulty, and places the spectator in an unusual and disconcerting relationship of ambivalence with the main protagonists.

This transgressive feature is less explicit in many of the earlier films, where the characters tend to be less fully drawn as potential social hazards, and more as simply self-interested wayward individuals, lacking in moral self-control. What is expressed in films like *Les Valseuses, Calmos, Préparez vos mouchoirs* and *La Femme de mon pote* is a hedonistic impulse which results in what might be termed anti-social acts, and is expressed through a ludic focus on male character interaction. This movement from an interest in tendencies in the early films, towards an exploration of explicit social contravention in the later works, reflects in Blier's corpus a development of the exploration of the carnivalesque as a mainly ludic concept, to that of the carnival as the locus of coherent and consistent popular tropes, of which trangression is one key element.

The application of a carnivalesque reading to Blier's work is immediately striking in *Les Valseuses*, arguably Blier's most groundbreaking film. *Les Valseuses* was conceived by Blier as a deliberate affront to good taste, and demonstrated open hostility, ideological and more importantly aesthetic, to the prevailing cultural point of view. As he has stated 'Il y avait encore des séquelles de mai '68 ... *Les Valseuses*, c'était un film contre la société. On attaquait tout à l'époque parce que ça faisait du bien. On tapait sur tout: la société, la famille. Il fallait pouvoir traiter son père de con!' (Halberstadt and Moriconi, 79).[2] Other films of the period were as aggressively conceived, but few if any had the visual and dramatic impact of *Les Valseuses*,[3] and what we see in Blier's work, both in and after *Les Valseuses*, is a constant reworking of this ambivalent anarcho-comic system of images, conveying criticism of the social order, while simultaneously functioning to create a tone of festivity and moral and social liberation.

Much of the deviant behaviour that the spectator and the diegetic community witness in this film has an explicitly sexual dimension, seeking deliberately to disrupt normal patterns of social interaction, by forging male–female or male–male relationships based primarily or wholly on sexual activity. Jean-Claude and Pierrot are characters who privilege and nurture, within an essentially comic framework, the sexual dimension of their lives, and who move towards establishing their own new society where they live out, in dramatic, if not narrative harmony, the experience

2 'This was still in the aftermath of May '68 ... *Les Valseuses* was a film against society. At that time, everything came under attack, because it felt good to attack. Everything was fair game: society, family. You had to be able to call your father a prick!'

3 Other strikingly unconventional films of the period include Marco Ferreri's *La grande bouffe* (1973) and Jean Eustache's *La Maman et la putain* (1973).

of their sexuality. They are driven by a hedonism which aims at material and physical gratification above all else (cars, clothes, food and sex are all objects of attraction for these characters), and this sets them apart from their wider society where pleasure and leisure are regarded as being secondary to the impulses towards production and self-control, impulses which are represented in the recurrent authoritarian partriarchal figures of policemen, prison warders, shop managers and bourgeois businessmen. This hedonistic desire is further intensified in the multiplication effect created by the consistent pairing in the film of the principal male characters: the comic paralleling and actions of dramatic synchronisation that result from this pairing, cast against the individual stasis of these figures of authority, work to reinforce both the effect of difference and exclusion from the norm in society, and the expression of transgressive desires.

This key notion of trangression in dramatic action and character construction is both retained and intensified in a film like *Tenue de soirée*. The central character of Bob, the bisexual seducer, is overtly deviant, as is his sexual appetite. Along with the other central characters, he engages in criminal activity such as burglary, theft and prostitution, and has relationships with 'shady' secondary characters, who themselves reinforce his deviance (homosexual clients, transvestites, pimps). The marital relationship which he disrupts in the course of the film is equally a travesty of the norm, characterised from the opening scene by a high degree of physical and verbal abuse, which goes on to permeate all relationships in the film.

The aim of the central protagonist is clearly stated as transgressive, that is the physical and emotional seduction of the character Antoine, and this is conveyed in the film through the development of a notion of excess which is itself encoded in the wider action of the narrative. For example, part of Bob's appeal to both the couple he seduces, and to the spectator, is located in the verbal virtuosity, rhetoric, *jeux de mots*, and rhythms in language which he constructs, all of which function to undermine patterns of normal or ordinary speech and communication. The effect of rapidity and accumulation which this engenders is evidence of excess, or transgression beyond the conventional parameters of cinematic discourse, and is appealing in both its qualities of emotional compulsion and comic appeal. This is demonstrated in the scene where the three break into a bourgeois household and dine on stolen *foie gras* and Pommard. The dramatic mechanisms of play are first comically retained in the rapid horizontal movement on the castored stools, and in the contrasting vertical movements and varying heights of the three characters. The range and spatial quality of the dramatic configuration is very Beckettian, recalling in particular the scene in Act 2 of *Waiting for Godot* where the characters engage in an activity of hat swapping (Beckett 1952: 101–2) and there is a clear comic slapstick dimension to the ritualised choreography of the action. This playful dimension expressed in the performance is reinforced in the attitudes adopted by Bob and Monique towards Antoine, who is excessively teased and cruelly humiliated in a way typical of the treatment of the carnival victim.

The scene features a very forceful use of language, again typical of the excesses of carnivalesque verbal expression: insofar as it explicitly uses the terms of reference of sexual activity, and does not sanitise in any way the expression, it takes on the function that Stam has described in relation to the carnival, which adopts a

> perspective on language which valorizes the obscene, the nonsensical and 'marketplace speech' as expressive of the linguistic creativity of the common people ... a rejection of social decorum entailing a release from oppressive etiquette, politeness, and good manners. (Stam 1992: 94)

In this scene, what we witness is the debasement of spiritual ideals through explicitly bawdy humour, characteristic of the carnival expression (Bob suggests that Antoine's penis is erect 'comme un jésus qui sort du four' ('like a sausage (called a 'jesus') hot from the oven') and an accumulative wordplay on culinary terms to denote Bob's sexual intentions towards Antoine: 'passer à la casserole'('screw' but emphasis on the casserole – cooking pot), 'rouleau de printemps' ('spring roll'), 'boudin' ('black pudding'), 'chocolat' ('chocolate'), 'patauger dans la semoule' ('wading through semolina'), 'ramonage de boyaux' ('sweeping out the guts'). This rapid, almost incoherent commentary by Bob is accompanied by an increasingly raucous belly laugh from Monique, who is positioned within the scene as the spectator for whose benefit the 'performance' is played. The vulgarity, profanity and general bawdy wordplay of the scene are key features of popular festive communication, that denies a place to the bourgeois social etiquette that is more conventionally a feature of cinematic seduction. Yet, paradoxically, there is also a Beckettian quality to the language in its emphasis on the poetry of the language at the heart of this: the sounds accumulate poetically in Bob's declamatory 'charrier', 'rier', 'eh ...' – (wordplay on the sounds of 'charrier' – 'to kid someone') and again in his summarising association of Pommard (the stolen wine), with 'braquemart' ('dick') and 'canular' ('hoax').[4] Ultimately, the transgressive elements at the heart of the scene function as an innovative display of linguistic creativity rather than as a trigger for total narrative rupture.

On another level, narrative excess in *Tenue de soirée* is firmly encoded in notions of display, and exhibition of the sexual impulse, and this is located principally in the character of Bob, who is seen in a variety of states of dress and undress, and ends the film in a state of flamboyant transvestism. The question of looking at what is being displayed is explored in a series of scenes, including the scene where Monique dresses in front of the men, the scene where the pimp arrives to watch Bob and Antoine make love, and the scene which follows on from that described above where the bourgeois couple demand participative sex from the three housebreakers (see p. 80). This transgressive discourse of 'looking and being looked at', especially as the action relates to characters dominating and inflicting humiliation on other characters, is a characteristic and recurrent feature of Blier's work, and one that draws on the carnivalesque model.

Much of the transgressive carnivalesque spirit of Rabelais'

---

4 A poetic effect is conveyed through similar devices of repetition in Beckett's drama. See for example the build up of sounds in 'elles chuchotent ... elles murmurent ... elles bruissent ... elles murmurent', or again in 'de plumes ... de feuilles ... de cendres ... de feuilles' (Beckett 1952: 88).

work as discussed by Bakhtin, is conveyed by appetite, whether this be sexual, material, verbal or oral. Qualities of excess and abundance have traditionally found expression through the reuniting of the community around the ceremonial action of feasting: in the cinema, for example, the notion of the dinner table as the place where primitive instinct meets civilized behaviour has been taken up by directors such as Luis Buñuel (*Le Charme discret de la bourgeoisie*, 1972) and Peter Greenaway (*The Cook, the Thief, his Wife, her Lover*, 1989). As Stam points out

> Rabelaisian imagery is ... intimately linked to the topos of the banquet, of the feast as temporary transfer to a utopian world of pleasure and abundance. Banquet imagery plays a primordial role in Rabelais, where virtually every page alludes to food and drink. (Stam 1992: 87)

Dramatic action in Blier's narratives is frequently related to the sharing or consumption of food (*Tenue de soirée, Trop belle pour toi, Préparez vos mouchoirs, Les Valseuses, Buffet froid*) and these scenes are always expressive of some kind of excessive emotion or heightened sensibility. The tone of misrule, which both defines the carnival and characterises Blier's work, often emerges from a scene of dining or eating, and thus the dramatic linking of this carnival trope with the excesses and transgressions of carnival practices is made explicit in the films.

A powerfully comic example of this is found in *Préparez vos mouchoirs* – a particularly carnivalesque film in its ludic dimension – in the scene in the dining room at the *colonie de vacances* (holiday camp). The transgressive action focuses on the character Christian, who, in the course of the scene, becomes the target of violence and assault. Evidence that the dramatic action has been constructed as carnivalesque is signalled in a series of dramatic elements: the procession of singing adults and children that announces the scene, the positioning of the significantly named Christian at the head of the procession, the ceremonial qualities of the meal and the mock reverence with which the moment of anticipated consumption is endowed. In a typically carnivalesque gesture, this ceremonial moment of reverence is comically undercut by the waiter's casual smoking of a cigarette, and by his moment of clearly nervous hesitation before presenting the foodstuffs to the predatory community.

In a dramatic exploration of 'the perennial carnival trope of the *puer-rex* (boy-king)' (Stam 1992: 113), Christian is singled out by the camera as the object of community scrutiny, and as the character who will become the object of the carnival's attentions. Gradually, the assault begins as the other boys begin to use their desserts as weapons against Christian. This is comically deflected in the fact that he is assaulted with *petits suisses*: no physical hurt or damage is implied, or indeed intended in the action of the assault, and it is thus symbolically bound to images of the fairground, and to slapstick activity. Yet, Christian's decision to move to the front of the crowd, and to place himself directly in the line of attack with the words 'puisqu'il vous faut une tête de Turc' ('since you need a whipping boy'), sees him adopting the symbolic role of the carnival effigy (anticipated in his place at the head of the pro-cession), and then assuming his function as such. In sanctioning the attack, Christian ultimately takes upon himself – from within the community itself – the expression of excess of the community, and the liberation of the energies of the crowd, in a fundamentally carnivalesque gesture. Symbolically, he becomes the carnival's representative individual, willingly assuming the role of the figure who is punished by, and on behalf, of all participants.

In a development of a further carnival trope, that of the *puer-senex* or child-man, this action is played out before an audience of adult spectators who do nothing, refusing their assigned roles as implementers of authority. A playful dramatic inversion operates in the positioning of the adults as the putative actors who watch the spectators perform, and this is stressed in the spatial distribution of the room and the protagonists: the room is set like a stage with the three adults sitting on a raised platform at the front of the room, and the children and Christian below and in front of them. The adults remain passive for the duration of the scene, while the children mete out the punishment, and assume all responsibilty for the development of the action. The male characters' eventual instruction to Christian to 'démaquille-toi' ('take off your make-up') hints at a form of role-play, leading onto the dramatic exploration of the child-man trope: Christian accepts the events and his role in them without question, and his rational, unemotional explanation to the adults of the significance of what has taken place, is a further example of the inversions of logic and commonplace behaviour which structure this film. The order which has been first inverted, then subverted in terms of the material environment, is subsequently intensified in the juvenile qualities of the two male adults whose reactions are comically juxtaposed with the intellectual maturity of the adolescent boy. Stéphane's speech to the assembled children before the arrival of the *petits suisses* is incongruous in its undue formality and eloquence, and is comically pitched at an inappropriate level for addressing children. His subsequent inability to respond articulately when interrogated by Christian about his intelligence quotient is therefore all the more ironic and amusing. This type of role reversal is an integral part of the carnival, and is indissociable from the concept of subversion of authority. In this scene, the sexual authority of the adult males is challenged by the boy, whom we see beginning to exert an authority over the adult woman (Carole Laure); this is hinted at in the final shot, which sees a wistful exchange of looks between the two, and is confirmed for both the spectator and the male protagonists, now relegated to being spectators of the action, in the scenes that follow.

In *Buffet froid*, the very title of the film focuses on food, and food works as a metaphor for the alliance of subversive behaviour and corrupt characters that structures the film. The alliance of the marginalised or criminal elements is built around food and the sharing of wine, as demonstrated in an early scene which takes place in Alphonse Tram's appartment: at the first meeting between Tram and his wife's killer, food is offered and shared, before the inspector arrives with a further contribution of wine. The *témoin* (witness), who then comes to request that Tram now murder him, is also offered wine, regardless of the sinister reasons for his visit. The sharing of food and wine that takes place in this scene transgresses all barriers imposed by society, represented by the policeman–murderer relationships, and by moral behaviour, seen in the murderer–husband of murdered woman and the killer–witness liaisons. The sharing of food here, then, signals the transgressive behaviour which brings the diverse social elements together, and anticipates the sense of illogicality of the subsequent events in the film.

In *Tenue de soirée*, the sharing of food, in this case stolen food, is also linked explicitly with the excesses of carnival practices. The bourgeois couple who arrive home in the sequence which directly follows that discussed above (see p. 76), express a different, but related form of transgressive appetite, and seek sexual recompense from the convivial criminals who have invaded their home. They seek sexual thrills to counter the boredom which they experience in a life where *foie gras* and Pommard are readily available, and endeavour to conjure up a moment of alternative excess on their own terms. As the orgy is proposed, and the bourgeois couple explicitly seek sexual thrills from those cast as 'lower orders', we are aware of the functioning of a salacious inversion at a level which transcends the dramatic action: the direct request for deviant sexual gratification has enormous impact, located as it is within an expression of dubious bourgeois morality, rather than within the actions of the central transgressive trio, who indeed express reluctance at extending their transgression to orgy. Given that the incitement to act in this way is driven by the imposition of authority, rather than by any general sense of carnivalesque misrule, the compulsion to act in a way that is not spontaneous inevitably results in a moment of genuine misrule, and the scene cuts to an aftermath suggestive of violence, assault and disruption of order, in which the furniture has been upturned, the bourgeois are unconscious, the trio are in a state of undress, and property has clearly been destroyed. In juxtaposing the two scenes in this way, the critical distance between the positive potential of subversive carnivalesque transgression, and the negative aspects of criminal or controlled transgression – the abuse of authority – is acknowledged in Blier's dramatic construction.

In Blier's work, excess and extravagance are transgressive concepts in that they allow for the overstepping of the normal confines of social activity and interaction, and pose a threat to the otherwise stable ordering of society. Yet, the food-based scenes, the crowds, the frantic sexual activity, even the absurd material acquisitions of Raoul and Stéphane in *Préparez vos mouchoirs*, are all invested with a degree of extravagance which is ultimately affirmative, dynamic and vital in the context of a carnivalesque reading of the narratives. Indeed, what Blier's dramatic style conveys repeatedly and very effectively, is the carnivalesque exhibition of an extraordinary degree of emotional or physical presence, a degree which extends beyond the norm, but which is inherently positive within this established popular context of hierarchical, social and behavioural inversions.

The utopian urge

In his introduction to Stallybrass and White's chapter entitled 'Bourgeois Hysteria and the Carnivalesque' Simon During points out that

> For Bakhtin, carnival contained a utopian urge: it displaced, even inverted, the normal social hierarchies. Carnival was also a time which encouraged different bodily needs and pleasures from those called upon by the ordinary rhythm of labour and leisure. (During 1993: 284)

The 'utopian urge' that During identifies as an intrinsic element in the construction of carnivalesque expression is, as we see here, founded on notions of displacement and inversion as they relate to the community experience of social, political and physical interaction. In other words, the nature of habitual or normal social organisation is challenged by the experience of carnival, which seeks to legitimise different patterns of social order and community interaction. Richard Dyer, in his article 'Entertainment and Utopia' (During 1993: 272–83), has examined how these codes of displacement and inversion function at the level of cinematic representation, which does not tend to present 'models of utopian worlds', but rather 'presents ... what utopia would feel like rather than how it would be organised' (During 1993: 273). In his discussion of the musical genre, Dyer examines the function of both representational signs such as stars, characters and places, and non-representational signs such as colour, texture, movement, rhythm, melody and camerawork, with regard to the creation of a 'utopian sensibility' in entertainment. Commenting on this, Robert Stam has suggested that

> The musical comedy can be seen as a two-dimensional carnival in which the oppressive structures of everyday life are not so much overturned (as in Bakhtin's conception) as they are stylized, choreographed, and mythically transcended ... Richard Dyer's analysis ... of the Hollywood musical as performing an artistic 'change of signs' whereby the negatives of social existence are turned into the positives of artistic transmutation strikingly parallels Bakhtin's account of carnival. For Dyer, the musical offers a utopian world characterized by 'energy' (for Bakhtin, carnival's gestural freedom and effervescence of dance and movement), 'abundance' (in carnival, omnipresent feasting, the fat of Mardi gras), 'intensity' (in carnival, the heightened theatricality of an alternative, 'second' life), 'transparency' (carnival's 'free and familiar contact'), and 'community' (carnival as loss of self, collective *jouissance*). (Stam 1992: 92–3)

An analysis of this kind, focusing on the dramatic components of narrative construction, and the artistic inversion of negative aspects of social practice,[5] provides a useful starting point for considering how a coherent concept of utopianism is created and explored in Blier's films from, and including, *Les Valseuses*. It will be argued here that Blier's dramatic conception envisions the same type of carnivalesque utopia as that described above, insofar as the dominant narrative techniques employed by Blier result in the same assertion of a fundamental expression of the concept of community, through the dramatic portrayal of social interaction, loss of self and processes of societal transformation.

The carnival and its theatrical derivatives are differentiated from other performative dramatic arts in the way in which they simultaneously involve and express notions of community. Carnival's distinctive expression depends on an absence of the spectator–performer barriers common to conventional institu-

---

5 The elements that characterise this 'utopian world' are defined by Dyer as responses to 'specific inadequacies in society', categorised by him as follows: 'scarcity, exhaustion, dreariness, manipulation, fragmentation' (During 1993: 278).

tionalised theatrical performance, and its purpose is to unite community members in a shared moment of collective liberty through verbal and physical expression. These are the features that modern *création collective* sought to emulate and explore in the central dramatic mechanism of the promenade performance, and which apply to *théâtre populaire*'s wider critique of the traditional passivity of the individual spectator.

One of the most effective and fundamental dramatic expressions of community in the carnival rites was to be found in the procession, the most significant of which was always that at the end of the carnival festivities, where crowds would follow the figure of *le roi carnaval*, the monarchical effigy that would be punished for his, and the crowd's, transgressions. This ritual procession has survived in carnival until the present day, and it remains inherently theatrical in the way in which it co-ordinates mass action: it combines the action of spectating with that of participation, as crowds follow, usually to a town square, in order to watch the carnival effigy being burned. This has an immense symbolic significance, as the humiliation and sacrifice of the representative figure atone for the faults of the society, and thus simultaneously liberate and renew the community as a whole.

This type of procession is central to the dramatic expression of the carnival experience as defined by Bakhtin and other scholars because of the particular emphasis that it gives to solidarity, shared activity, and implicitly, intra-societal communication. An assumption of disguise frequently accompanied this representation of community life, a theatrical device which functioned to further erode the external trappings of social hierarchy and thereby contributed to the dismantling of the social barriers of age, class and profession. The gathering of individuals in common purpose, so fundamental to the carnival rites, was thus advanced along egalitarian lines, by a willing concealment of the outward signs of social and economic status. The levelling of individuals at which this self-consciously dramatic procession aimed, sought to widen, albeit temporarily, the social base of community, and constituted, on a basic level, an enabling and intensely utopian liberation from the dominant social order.

Furthermore, the representation in the carnival rites of physical interaction, taking the form most commonly of a libertarian dramatisation of sexual activity and the processes of reproduction, is evidence of a fascination with the nature and processes of instinct and renewal as they relate to the health of the community. The role of the female as the source of reproduction was celebrated in the carnival, traditionally a springtime festival, and rebirth and transformation of self are thus potent carnivalesque concepts, which signify the means by which the individuals in society renew the whole. Thus, a concern with the elemental or organic aspects of the fertile human body, aspects which, in isolation, have no value, and indeed express a negative value of impotence, is further evidence of a profoundly utopian urge at the heart of the carnival expression.

All Blier's major films display dramatic associations with, and frequently incorporate explicit re-enactments of, the symbolic rites of the carnival outlined above. The expression of community or shared experience at the heart of the carnival is a constant feature of his work, and is represented through a variety of dramatic and cinematic mechanisms which include the privileging of duos and trios of characters, the action of procession or pursuit, the presence of an integrated spectator, moments of direct address to camera, and the exploration of techniques of mediated narration. There are recurrent shots of characters in identical dress, or in complementary poses, suggestive of an affirmation of a non-individual consciousness, and of a group or community co-ordinated reaction to events and situations. The ludic focus on sexual activity is significant insofar as it is represented as an end in itself, without natal consequence, and there is typically a multiple or public dimension to its presentation. The question of transformation or recreation is fundamental to Blier's experimentation with notions of gender performativity, and the destabilising effect of this, both as narrative form and as content image (involving costume, disguise, visual and verbal role-play) expresses the same utopian desire as in the carnival rites.

The predisposition in Blier's work towards patterns of groups, crowds, couples, and trios, is evidence of a dramatic rendering of the carnivalesque concept of the community experience. As we have seen, the absence of the individual, and the concentration on the individual only in relation to those with whom he or she interacts implicit in this dramatic patterning, results in the expression, characteristic of Blier's work, of the shared rather than the isolated in human existence. The focus on multiple or mass action, and the tendency towards techniques of accumulation of characters in the course of the narratives, is evidence of an implicit building of social units contained in the dramatic action of the films. All Blier's films display this pattern of accumulation, whereby one or two characters join with others who then remain with the original group throughout the course of the film (*Les Valseuses, Préparez vos mouchoirs, La Femme de mon pote, Tenue de soirée, Mon homme*), or they display patterns of accumulation which are integral to the wider dramatic action (e.g. *Calmos, Notre histoire, Un deux trois soleil*). Group formation is a recurrent and cinematically original feature in Blier's system of images: crowds of onlookers frequently gather, or follow or observe passively a moment of unfolding action. Although this is in the main a disconcerting presence for the viewer, due largely to its unrealistic nature, it can work to comic effect, and the comic potential of this technique is explored in *Buffet froid* when the police arrive to look for the violinist in the tower block. The extravagance of the pursuing – legitimised – crowd, and the farcical dimension to their movement within the tower and on the stairs, is in stark contrast to the lack of pursuit, and indeed the acceptance of the assassin of Madame Tram.

A clear pattern of character accumulation underlies the narrative structure of *Les Valseuses*, determining both the action and the outcome of events, and this is portrayed through a motif of pursuit and avoidance by individuals, representatives of authority, and explicitly drawn crowds, and by the formation and reformation of the central character group. Relatively minor transgression without significant consequence in the narrative is comically deflated by a reaction of pursuit: the initial terrorising of Suzanne/Ursula and the stealing of her handbag sees Jean-Claude and Pierrot pursued by a crowd of workers, and then by the men whose bicycles they steal in order to make good their escape. They are later pursued by police officers on motorcycles, by the driver of a combine harvester, and by a supermarket manager, all to comic effect. They themselves in turn pursue Marie-Ange, who becomes a part of the central group, Jeanne as she leaves the prison, and later Jacques, Jeanne's criminal son, who is also approached as he leaves prison. The latter two characters temporarily become part of the continuously renewed social unit, as is demonstrated in the dinner scene with Jacques at the rural cottage beside the river. In this way, the desire of these marginal characters to create, live and interact within social systems is clearly located at the heart of the film's narrative. It is significant that more serious misdemeanours in the narrative events, such as the shooting of the prison guard by Jacques, are accorded a less comic treatment than those described above, and feature a pursuit of menace and danger, enhanced in this case by darkness and brooding music, signalling the definitive exclusion of a protagonist from this community. In this instance, Jean-Claude and Pierrot are accomplices to the act, but not the perpetrators, therefore the anticipated punishment is unjustified, and outwith the parameters of the carnival. Their own misdemeanors are less serious and less transgressive by comparison.

Given the fundamentality within the carnival of the displacement of normal social hierachies in order to facilitate communication within an otherwise socially diverse community, related questions about the nature of social interaction, or communication across social divisions, are central to a carnivalesque reading of Blier's thematic structure. Indeed, *Les Valseuses* concentrates almost exclusively on the issue of failure of communication, particularly within the male community: there is little male communication across age, profession or social status, and this is achieved only within the narrow confines of the modern male social experience, as exemplified by the successful, but emotionally limited, Jean-Claude–Pierrot relationship. The older bourgeois male characters express none of the sense of liberation from social constraint necessary to the sound functioning of their society: the supermarket manager, doctor, and petit-bourgeois father are all materialistic, socially conditioned, and, as such, stand in dramatic contrast with the free-thinking, morally neutral, picaresque Jean-Claude and Pierrot. Hence, the social crisis which appears to be embodied in the characters of the two delinquents, and upon which contemporary critics concentrated a great deal, is in fact located elsewhere in the male characterisations: this is a society already in crisis, where male communication is a small-scale and relatively ephemeral condition. Alternatively, what is lacking from the male experience is the expression of the carnival, which liberates and permits communication where none generally takes place. Despite the upbeat tone of the film, and the very positive suggestion of the possibility of valid exchange between modern – young – men and women, *Les Valseuses* is a film about lack and frustration rather than about communication and fulfilment. Interestingly, this failure to interact in a liberating way is subsequently countered by the male characters in *Buffet froid* where the film functions around extreme and intense communion between socially incongruous males. Furthermore, the female experience is portrayed by Blier as essentially different: when female characters are brought together, even in opposition, as is the case in *Trop belle pour toi*, they are able to communicate authentically and profoundly with each other. The example of the participation of Marie-Ange in the sexual initiation of Jacqueline in *Les Valseuses*, is a powerful and symbolic example of this, as is the parallel example of the initiation of Camille by Joëlle in *Merci la vie*. The evidence that social difference is more easily overcome in the domain of female interaction is borne out by Blier's mature concentration on female relationships where he demonstrates the intensity and vital nature of communication in the female domain.

This failure to communicate, highlighted in *Les Valseuses*, and to which Blier returns frequently in his later films, is, however, a more complex issue than simply one of overcoming an implicit class-based social division. In carnivalesque interaction, the social merges with the physical, the sexual and the gendered to create a union which is utopian in its interrelation of elements. The difficulty of achieving this in anything other than a temporary state is apparent in the functioning of the male–female experience, which is complicated in Blier's films by a deep-rooted acknowledgement of difference, frequently translated into overt incomprehension: male–female relationships are fraught with anxiety and mis-understanding, and are largely unsuccessful in terms of establish-ing permanent unions. There is, however, periodic suggestion of achievement of meaningful exchange between the sexes, and in *Les Valseuses* this is powerfully demonstrated in the scenes of intense sexual and emotional communication between Jean-Claude, Pierrot and Jeanne. First, the male characters seek out a woman who is older than they are; she is therefore immediately identified as a more mature, and to a large extent more socially refined character than them, albeit with a criminalised tendency in common. But Jeanne, played by Jeanne Moreau provides also, very significantly, an important intertextual reference in that she is the iconic face of the desirable *nouvelle vague* female; her willing self-debasement here, her seduction at the hand of two boorish louts, therefore strikes at her own established image, and at the con-temporary conventions of female representation and performance.

The moment of real communication between the three comes in the love-making scene, which, unusually for Blier, has a highly eroticised perspective, focusing as it does on the conventional elements of underwear and facial expressions of pleasure. It is, in stark contrast to the previous comic three-in-a-bed scene with Marie-Ange, narrated with discretion and some modesty, and gives the sense of an intense, shared experience, without exploita-tion of one party by another, almost of a moment of communion between individuals. The shared experience is what dominates visually and emotionally, and there is a lyrical quality to the images filmed in close shot, and almost in slow motion. It is a temporary moment in the film, and an idealised, utopian view of sexual union within a group, but it is a profound moment of emotion, brutally undermined by the sudden violent suicide of Jeanne in the next scene. There is a bewildering destruction of the established communication, and a need to seek and renew the experience with another (Marie-Ange) immediately after. There are, then, levels of communication built up between male and female in this and subsequent films: communication is not taken as given, but evolves with the events. It is characteristic of Blier's work that there is no sanitising of the modern experience with regard to male–female relationships, but the problematic aspects of this are dramatically resolved within a carnivalesque framework which aims at communication across multiple social divides.

A desire to express and capture dramatically the regenerative nature of the female is central to Blier's approaches to the representation of female presence and to the portrayal of male–female relationships. This results in an intensely carnivalesque focus on the action of reproduction, and on human sexuality with respect to the process of reproduction. *Préparez vos mouchoirs* is a film about fertility–infertility, sexual potency–impotence, and the desire for physical regeneration, and this sexual dimension underlines all the narrative events; the elusive realities of procreation and birth which are pursued in the film, are ultimately exchanged for that of symbolic rebirth as Solange, and her fertility, are reinvented by the narrative events. *Un deux trois soleil* returns to this theme, locating the symbolic force of regeneration in the earth mother figure, and in the nature of the close inter-generational community experience. The film is permeated by a sense of energetic, joyful activity in the midst of ordinary life, with many of the images focusing on relations between adults and children, or on adults as children engaged in play. There are repeated liberating images of openness, which relate directly to the urban environment: doors are not closed, people go in and out of each other's houses, space is afforded by the vast wastelands which surround the *cité*. This mood of liberation is intensified in the elements of music, colour and lighting, evident in the rai soundtrack, the predominance of bright primary colours and multicolouring, and in the emphatic presence of the Marseille sun.[6]

The symbolism of a more primitive community spirit is intensified in the overtly exotic character of Gladys, the black woman who, in an early scene from the film, is shown engaged in actions of mothering, reviving and protecting. A child is accidentally shot

---

6 This recalls Dyer's analysis of the non-representational aspects that contribute to the creation of a utopian perception at the level of the emotions. Dyer (1981: 273–4).

by a pursuing policeman, and the policeman gives an instruction that the boy should be taken to his wife for attention. Gladys, a physically large woman begins the process of 'réchauffement' ('warming up'), as she terms it, by removing her clothes and placing the injured boy across her breasts. She is surrounded by a public of young boys and Victorine, the community that constitutes an extension of the spectating audience. Intimate camerawork places the spectator in close proximity to the action, associating him or her spatially with the point of view of Victorine.

A sharing of experience is again what dominates visually and emotionally in this scene. On the one hand, there is a sense that the participants have designated roles in this ritualistic action – to spectate, perform or interrogate – and the lack of inhibition and surprise at what ensues suggests a normalised public dimension to the act. Significantly, the shared experience dominates most forcefully in the female sphere, as the instructions and explanations are addressed directly from Gladys to Victorine (and the camera), whereas the boys are instructed to be quiet, and are excluded other than as observers of the action. The portrayal of a degree of ritualised activity in the midst of ordinary life in this scene produces the heightened dramatic mood that is a characteristic feature of Blier's films.

There is, then, in this scene, a symbolic union of concepts of motherhood, femaleness, fertility and sex. A fundamental link is made between the woman's body and the health of the community, and, in the action of the woman's body imitating the act of lovemaking, of the potential of sex as a regenerative, renewing force. It is significant that when, in a variation on this scene, Victorine herself takes on a parallel role of nurturer or life-giver at the end of the film, the marked absence of a visibly maternal body means that the action is viewed less comfortably, and is a more ambiguous representation of the processes of carnivalesque regeneration which the film has explored. Laughter, in this first scene, comes with the confusion between the pleasure taken by the sexually precocious adolescent boys at their proximity to the mature female sexual body, and their desire, as young children, for the comfort implicit in the maternal body: one boy's question, 'je pourrais passer aussi, si jamais je suis blessé?' ('can I call in too, if I'm ever hurt?), voices this confusion for the spectator, and thereby comically undercuts a moment of intense emotional engagement. This provocative portrayal of male characters instinctively associating the elements and processes of female nurturing with sexual gratification is found elsewhere in Blier's films. In *Les Valseuses*, for example, Jean-Claude and Pierrot instinctively associate the functioning of the elements and processes of female reproduction with sexual gratification, as is evident in the scene on the train with the breast-feeding mother. In so doing, they re-enact the rites of carnival where males take pleasure in seeking to identify their sexual function. For the spectator, however, the confusion of maternal physicality with the action of sexual activity is disorientating, and arguably all the more disturbing given the clear exertion of strength of will and free choice on the part of the female character.

The film *Un deux trois soleil* makes much of the fluidity of the woman and mother within the community, with the interchangeability of the female characters at different points in the narrative allowing for the arguably regressive identification of woman, in an essentialist way, as a presence rather than an individual. She is positioned, however, as central and powerful in the functioning of the community, further evidence of Blier's according of value rather than negation to her presence. The family, of which she is traditionally the centre, is also represented as interchangeable in this film, a device which complements Blier's thematic interrogation of the concept of family as community. In this way, patterns of unfixed characterisation, and the inevitably incoherent narrative structures that these bring about, result in an unequivocally utopian expression of the organic community.

The concept of transformation is, as we have already seen in our discussion of the grotesque body, a major element of the carnival experience, and this is true both with respect to the question of inhabitual performed action on the part of the individual, and to that of renewal or rebirth of the wider community. As Stam has stated

> the Bakhtinian trope of the 'nonfinalizability' of human character and meaning recalls Nietzsche's Dionysus as the embodiment of the eternally creative principle, forever exulting in the transformation of appearances ... What Nietzsche values in the Dionysian experience is the transcendence of the individuating ego, led to feel a euphoric loss of self as it is subsumed into a larger philosophical whole. (Stam 1992: 89)

This process of renewal through transformation, and subsequent consumption by the wider body, is expressive of a utopian urge which aims at social integration and an acknowledgement by the community of its own organic nature.

In *Les Valseuses*, the young men, although they do not evolve as characters, are in fact transformed by their experiences: they are shown in the final scene as unthreatening, carefree and quite likeable, which they have not always been in the course of the film. This is suggested by Marie-Ange's total ease with them, and by the harmonious combination of movement and music: the swaying rhythm of both the car and the camera create an impression of gliding and weightlessness, and the diegetic and non-diegetic sound are harmoniously – and festively – united in the musical soundtrack. The film ends on a utopian moment whereby the sexual and physical excesses of the male protagonists have been tamed; the animal instincts have been first satisfied, then controlled, ultimately presenting no further threat to the wider society. In this film, as in the popular festive tradition, a different type of man emerges from the first: a more mature, sated, adult man; the male is unmasked, only to show that he is what he always seemed to be underneath, and what we, the spectators, have had privileged glimpses of throughout the film. This is prefigured by the sexual initiation of Jacqueline, which is also a moment of utopian transformation; it takes on an almost ritualistic dimension, with the slow, deliberate participation of both male and female characters in the female rite of passage. What we witness is a scene of transformation, in the public, shared domain; it is filmed in close shot, with all four characters variously in the frame. The mood is consensual, joyful, participatory, and it is significant that we do not see the sex act, only an expression of pleasure, trust and discovery, even if this remains relatively codified in terms of the representation of female reactions to sex in film. This transformation of the girl into the woman is introduced into the action as something that crucially equips the individual for life in society, and results in both renewal and independence: the four characters all embrace, and the trio leave Jacqueline by the side of the road, moving onwards, but in a different direction from themselves.

Tenue de soirée is, on one level, about sexual transformation, and on another about processes of reassessment within individual and group consciousnesses. The visual impact of the film is of course derived from the external physical transformations that take place, first in terms of the environment and lifestyle of Antoine and Monique, but second as a consequence of the developing relationship of Antoine and Bob. All narrative and plot developments are related to the urge to transform and renew: the stagnation of a relationship at the outset, the sexual boredom of the pimp who buys Antoine, the stifling domesticity of the Bob–Antoine relationship, which brings about Antoine's transvestism, and the evolving dress and domiciles of the main characters. The enactment of the practice of transvestism serves, as in the carnival tradition, to release the characters from 'the burden of socially imposed sex roles' (Stam 1992: 93), and thereby actively subverts the hegemonic ordering of gender difference. The film deals explicitly and provocatively with notions of hierarchical and high cultural inversion; Bob's statement to Antoine that 'je ferai de toi une reine' ('I'll turn you into a queen'), hints at the final scenes of the film in which Antoine is reinvented as the queen Antoinette. The allusion to a problematic historical figure,[7] and the rejection of the double notion of kingship (physical manhood and male authority), present a debasement of cultural assumptions which goes beyond the explicit travesty of societal norms explored in the sexual relationships and dress codes of the two characters. The reversal of orders of gender implicit in Antoine and Bob's transvestism is a feature of carnival which is indicative of a subversive

7 Lynne Hunt raises many questions about Marie-Antoinette including that of her alleged 'sexual depravity' in Hunt (1992).

attitude to matters of authority and order, yet the excessive theatricality of the final scene points not to a permanent condition, but rather to moments 'out of time', thereby reinforcing the structuring utopian urge of the films.

Utopianism, in Blier's films, as in the popular festive tradition, can be read as an attempt to assert the legitimacy of social, sexual, physical and gender relations which the cultural hegemony deems to be in some way menacing, excessive or deviant. This endeavour to 'rewrite the rules' or construct anew, is expressed through the imagery and key dramatic mechanisms of the films, and is reflected in the narrative construction in a relative lack of respect for the traditional dramatic unities of time, space and action: often the period of time in which the action takes place is unclear, locations change frequently, the action is elliptically narrated, giving a sense of rapidity and accumulation to the unfolding events. Blier's films reject modernist notions of psychological scrutiny – indeed, comic deflation of moments of emotional intensity is a common dramatic mechanism in Blier's films – and instead seek to portray the individual as motivated by more primitive, elemental or, indeed, popular impulses. Blier's dramatic exploration of concepts of participatory action, physical dialogue, sexual potency and collective regeneration, and the inversions of normal order that these engender, are all evidence of a dramatic conception which acknowledges the popular festive traditions, and which engages fully with their dominant expressive forms.

The politics of carnival

Given that the period of Blier's first major commercial successes was the early 1970s, and given the predominance of carnivalesque forms in the films, it is possible to read Blier's work as a considered post-1968 expression of society, expressing the same elements of the utopian sensibility of entertainment defined by Richard Dyer. The qualities of abundance, energy and community that Dyer identifies and explains as a reaction to scarcity, exhaustion and fragmentation in society, clearly have some historical application here, where the nature of the utopian or carnivalesque commentary is indissociable from the defining social and political events and youth culture of the late 1960s. Blier's films begin by dramatically examining the freedom and liberty that is part of the social and historical expression of the period, and he succeeds in retaining a sense of the mythology of this, for him, seminal period, in his mature film-making. The focus across the body of his work is not so much class-based, as is conventional in the political *théâtre populaire*, but is rather generational, as was the case in Parisian *café-théâtre*: there is a sense in the pattern of his films of an evolving assessment of this generation (*les soixante-huitards*) which, in France, defined itself in a moment of social carnival. Indeed, Blier's thematic and dramatic conception has very much evolved with his audience; his box-office successes over the period of his film-making reflect cultural identification with a certain social group, reflecting their post-1968 dissent, their evolving experience of sexuality, emotional commitment and latterly middle age (or at least their distance from youth), and finally their mature concern with social issues of national and global significance. This evolution is reflected in the recurrence of a small number of leading actors across a wide body of work, resulting in a consistency of characterisation across roles, and is marked by the changing priorities of the main protagonists as they age. As Blier has remarked

> je crois qu'il y a des problèmes de génération: on a un certain âge à un certain moment, et il y a à cette époque-là toute une famille avec qui il faut tourner et d'autres avec qui il ne faut surtout pas, parce qu'ils sont trop vieux ou trop jeunes. (Toubiana 1988: 13)[8]

But more significant yet is the way in which Blier's work dramatically, more than thematically, takes up the popular insubordination that characterises this transitional period in French culture, and the way in which he realigns the mechanisms of popular dramatic expression in the cinema. His work retains the verbal

---

8 'I believe that there are generational problems: you're a certain age at a certain time, and thus there's a whole community you can work with, and others that you can't work with, because they're either too old or too young.'

and visual traditions of twentieth-century popular cinema – working-class heroes, urban milieux, verbal repartee, popular language – but forwards them in a way that is decisively post–1968 political. In the context of a failed social revolution, where the workers do not lead but follow, and where intellectual rather than popular elements set the agenda and terms of reference, Blier's return to very traditional, 'pre-cultural' or pre-discursive dramatic codes shows a desire to engage with the expression of the popular consciousness at a level other than the purely thematic.

Blier's work can usefully be considered within the tradition of carnivalesque folk culture in its range of manifestations detailed above, and it is directly related to the modern forms of this same culture in its dramatic association with the post-1968 Parisian *café-théâtre* and Brechtian stage theory. The tone of his parody is not purely satirical, and not purely about negation, inversion or *retournement* as Bakhtin understands modern formal parody,[9] but focuses on a revealing comic expression of a modern popular consciousness through a series of subversive attacks which take account of all of these codes. Blier's clear focus on aspects of life pertinent to the modern, and to a large extent universal, social experience, within a framework of carnivalesque observation and commentary is indicative of an attempt to acknowledge a former fundamental function of *la fête*, of which, as Alain Faure states 'il est naturel de retrouver au cœur de la fête ce qui était au fond de tous les bouleversements du moment: la remise en cause des inégalités, la contestation de l'ordre social.'[10] This corresponds to Bakhtin's view, documented by Stam, that 'carnival is more than mere festivity; it is the oppositional culture of the oppressed, the symbolic anticipatory overthrow of oppressive social structures' (Stam 1992: 173). Thus, Blier's appropriation of dramatic forms which explicitly demonstrate and celebrate social revolution,

9 'We must stress, however, that the carnival is far distant from the negative and formal parody of modern times. Folk humor denies, but it revives and renews at the same time. Bare negation is completely alien to folk culture' (Bakhtin 1984: 11).

10 'At the heart of *fête* one finds that which motivates all forms of social unrest: the calling into question of inequality, the challenging of the social order' (Faure 1978: 90).

associates his work on a further level with the *agit-prop* aims of modern Brechtian theatre, as well as with the spirit of contestation that was an intrinsic element of the post-1968 popular cultural apparatus and discourse. The sense of revival and renewal which his work dramatises, and the reversal of the rules of social logic that the characters express, are implicitly political, while the dismantling of culturally inscribed social and gendered orders is remarkable in the way in which it challenges ingrained perceptions of modern popular cultural expression as inherently apolitical.

References

Bakhtin, Mikhail (1984), *Rabelais and his World* (trans. Hélène Iswolsky), Bloomington: Indiana University Press.

Beckett, Samuel (1952), *En attendant Godot*, Paris, Editions de Minuit.

During, Simon (ed.) (1993), *The Cultural Studies Reader*, London and New York, Routledge.

Faure, Alain (1978), *Paris carême-prenant: Du carnaval à Paris au XIXe siècle 1800–1914*, Paris, Hachette.

Halberstadt, Michèle and Moriconi, Martine (1986), 'Le Perturbateur tranquille: entretien avec Bertrand Blier', *Première* 109, April.

Hayward, Susan (1996), *Key Concepts in Cinema Studies*, London and New York, Routledge.

Hunt, Lynne (1992), *The Family Romance of the French Revolution*, London, Routledge.

Perry, Sheila and Cross, Máire (1997), *Voices of France: Social, Political and Cultural Identity*, London, Pinter.

Stam, Robert (1992), *Subversive Pleasures: Bakhtin, Cultural Criticism and Film*, Baltimore, Johns Hopkins University Press.

Toubiana, Serge (1988), 'Josiane Balasko, Bertrand Blier: jeux de mots, jeux d'acteurs', *Cahiers du cinéma* 407–8, May.

1 The original trio: Patrick Dewaere, Miou-Miou and Gérard Depardieu as Pierrot, Marie-Ange and Jean-Claude in the riverside scene from *Les Valseuses*

2 Stéphane and Raoul (Dewaere and Depardieu) in *Préparez vos mouchoirs* relaxing at one of Blier's many rural retreats

3 Christian Belœil in the aftermath of the petits-suisses attack in *Préparez vos mouchoirs*. Left to right: Raoul (Depardieu), Stéphane (Dewaere), Christian (Riton) and Solange (Carole Laure)

4 Angelic looks from a devilish male trio: Alphonse Tram (Depardieu), l'inspecteur Morvandieu (Bernard Blier) and 'l'assassin' (Jean Carmet) surrounded by the forces of law and order in *Buffet froid*

5 Waiting for 'l'homme en bleu': re-enacting Beckett in *Buffet froid*. From left to right: Tram (Depardieu), l'inspecteur (Bernard Blier) and 'l'assassin' (Carmet)

6 The 'grotesque body': Coluche's comic celebrity is challenged in *La Femme de mon pote*

7 The art of seduction: Antoine (Blanc) and Bob (Depardieu) blend with their surroundings in *Tenue de soirée*

8 Monique (Miou-Miou), Antoine (Michel Blanc) and Bob (Depardieu) dine on stolen *foie gras* and Pommard in *Tenue de soirée*

9 A grotesque flourish in *Tenue de soirée*: a heavily made-up Antoine (Blanc) holds a bewigged Bob (Depardieu) hostage

10 The reappearance of the shopping trolley in *Merci la vie* launches Blier's 'second career' in the 1990s: Joëlle (Anouk Grinberg), the abandoned bride, is rescued by Camille (Charlotte Gainsbourg)

11 Joëlle (Grinberg) and Camille (Gainsbourg) usurp Blier's male predators in *Merci la vie*

12 Bertrand Blier on the set of *Un deux trois soleil*

4

Bending gender[1]

That Bertrand Blier is misogynistic in his film-making has increasingly come to be a given of Blier criticism and reviews. Indeed, in a review of Gaston Haustrate's monograph on Blier, published in the *French Review*, John Anzalone noted that 'with the exception of Eustache and Pasolini, Blier has probably produced more films deemed offensive than any other mainstream European director' (Anzalone, 1990). This offensiveness has frequently been equated with an expression of misogyny on the part of the director, which is seen as a reductive and aggressive attitude towards the female subject, and by extension the female spectator. There is considerable evidence, at least on a surface level, to support this view; what it fails to take account of, however, is that Blier's preferred modes of gender representation which, as we have seen, frequently result in unconventional male characterisation in the films, equally extend to female representation, and that these modes of representation, grounded as they are in established popular expressive forms, are intrinsic to Blier's key aim of the subversion of narrative and cultural assumptions about performance.

Blier's characteristic approach, and one which has earned him this reputation of a misogynist film-maker, is to work with outwardly conventional gendered roles which define the female subject in three key ways: by the image she projects, by her position with regard to the male subject and, most importantly, by the

1 An earlier version of this chapter appeared in *Bertrand Blier and Misogyny* (Harris and King 1996: 12–25).

nature of the action executed by the female subject and the influence of this on narrative organisation and development. Exactly why this should be construed as a particularly misogynistic treatment seems, on the surface, to be unproblematic: there is little in the portrayal and positioning of the female that seems to valorise the female subject: the control of women by exertion of male power, in both symbolic and active terms, appears to be translated into image and narrative form in Blier's work, and the recurrent physical and verbal violence perpetrated against the female subject arguably reinforces a simple and singularly unprogressive view of her as object and victim of male action and oppression. In this way, she is positioned in a secondary and frequently consenting role with regard to the male subjects. This is accentuated by a range of female performance characteristics – emotional passivity, physical inanimation and verbal uncommunicativeness – characteristics which are direct inversions of those held by the majority of Blier's male characters. Furthermore, the explicit sexuality of these female subjects, central to their identification in the narrative, is highlighted in the *mise-en-scène* and in the narrative action, working to confirm a highly conventional filmic view of the woman as one who assumes an active, and therefore guilty, role in the process of her own oppression. Joan Smith, in her writing on the subject of misogyny, advances the view that films that suggest that women in some way desire sexual violence legitimise the violence itself, and set in motion a complex process by which guilt at the action is transferred from the perpetrator to the victim (Smith 1989: 20), a process previously explored by Molly Haskell in her seminal text *From Reverence to Rape: the Treatment of Women in the Movies* (1974).

In short, Blier's work has been construed as misogynistic insofar as it appears to be unchallenging, conservative and accusatory in its treatment of the female subject. Yet an analysis of the complexities of female characterisation and narrative positioning in Blier's films reveals that where Blier initially appears to conform to a conventional ordering of image and position with regard to gender divisions in the narrative, with the mechanisms of performance reinforcing this apparent misogyny, it is the mechanisms of performance themselves that ultimately challenge the validity of a misogynistic reading of his work.

The emphasis on a high degree of physicality in representation is a common feature of the popular comic tradition within which Blier's work is constructed; the representation of the female in particular has long been codified in terms of her physical nature and by a particular association with what Bakhtin terms the 'material lower bodily stratum'. But, far from constituting an attack on female integrity, this tradition sees such a construction of body and character as a positive force in the carnivalesque processes of social renewal and emotional development. To return to Bakhtin's analysis we see that

> In reality, the popular comic tradition and the ascetic tradition are profoundly alien to each other. The popular tradition is in no way hostile to woman and does not approach her negatively. In this tradition woman is essentially related to the material bodily lower stratum; she is the incarnation of this stratum that degrades and regenerates simultaneously. She is ambivalent. She debases, brings down to earth, lends a bodily substance to things, and destroys; but, first of all, she is the principle that gives birth ... Womanhood is shown in contrast to the limitations of her partner (husband, lover or suitor); she is a foil to his avarice, jealousy, stupidity, hypocrisy, bigotry, sterile senility, false heroism, and abstract idealism ... She represents in person the undoing of pretentiousness, of all that is finished, completed, and exhausted. (Bakhtin 1984: 240)

As we see, the popular comic tradition actively celebrates female corporeality, focusing on the female body as an alternative to phallocentrism and to notions of dominant patriarchy. The female is here perceived in terms of ambivalent images, which, in their dependence on the material, physical body, are at odds with the positioning of women in more cultured literary traditions. Blier's gendered narrative ordering corresponds entirely to this popular dramatic frame of analysis in which the woman stands as a defining counterpoint to the foibles and inadequacies embodied in the male. His deliberate attempt to go beyond the conventional limits of gender representation – and the attack on the patriarchal norms of mainstream cinema that this implies – is a further important example of the many processes of narrative subversion that inform the films. His work conceals a daring assault on the common objectification of woman by the 'male gaze',[2] and the location of this subversion within the codes of female performance crucially problematises any reading of Blier's work as misogynistic.

The images that are characteristic of male and female inter- action in Blier's films frequently show men in verbal conflict with women, and men performing aggressive acts on women. These are unpleasant and often disturbing images for the spectator to deal with: the female body is made visible and scrutinised, and humiliation, denigration, and exclusion are the condition of the sexed–sexual female subject. The verbal vulgarity and aggressive behaviour on the part of men towards women is directly linked to the sexual identity of the female characters, and results in a pattern of abuse which targets and ultimately victimises the female spectator–witness by association. Examples of this kind of aggres- sion are extremely common in Blier's work, and their frequency has been part of the contention that surrounds them. Some of the most notorious – and disturbing – of these are to be found in the early comic films *Les Valseuses*, *Calmos* and *Préparez vos mouchoirs*.

In the first, a nursing mother, played by Brigitte Fossey is accosted on a train by the two male protagonists and offered money to allow one of them to suck in the baby's place. The woman, at first fearful, but increasingly compliant, agrees to the transaction and the activity envisaged by the two men takes place. Later in the film, a post-menopausal woman (Jeanne) just freed from years in prison is stalked by the two aggressors, and then shares a meal, and subsequently a night of love-making with them. The episode ends brutally when she commits suicide by shooting herself in the vagina. In *Calmos*, a desire for the company of men is expressed through an opening sequence of incredible female passivity, which concludes with a direct-to-camera–gynaecologist view of a woman

2 This is the narrative ordering identified by Laura Mulvey in her essay 'Visual Pleasure and the Narrative Cinema', originally published in *Screen* 16:3, autumn 1975, and reproduced in Mast *et al.* (1992). Subsequent page references refer to the latter text.

patient, naked with her legs in stirrups. The view of her lazily scratching her genital area is set against that of the gynaecologist who indifferently prepares a pâté sandwich before abandoning the woman in his surgery. Women in the film are increasingly cast as sexual predators, who hunt men like animals, and round them up like prisoners of war. The men, including the classic Blier duo in the second of its many manifestations, are ultimately destroyed by the sexually active female body, which devours them through the vagina. *Préparez vos mouchoirs*, scandalises from its opening restaurant scene in which a husband offers his wife to a complete stranger to see if the stranger can give her more sexual pleasure and make her pregnant. As in *Beau-père*, a few years later, the matter of adolescent sexuality is brought front of stage: here the wife is seduced not by the increasingly amorous lover, but by one of her holiday charges, a boy of 13. Their sexual union, as in *Beau-père*, takes place at the adolescent's insistence. This pattern of apparent denigration and devaluation continues throughout the films, until we arrive at the complex final cycle: in *Merci la vie* the woman has become the conduit for sexual disease, and *Mon homme* sees the prostitute Marie satisfying her maternal instincts through a willing prostitution.

These images would seem to bear out the assertion of one scholar who has sought to address the question of Blier's misogyny, that in the director's work there is a 'reduction of women to their genitals. Blier's female characters are defined solely in terms of their sexual organs and hence their sexual activity' (Rollet 1994: 241), and indeed it would seem that this sexual activity is further complicated by the way in which it is constructed to inspire disgust and rejection, rather than engagement or pleasure on the part of the spectator. In many cases, borne out by dialogue, female sexuality is associated with dirt or danger: something which threatens to contaminate or affect adversely in some way the male subject.[3]

3 Rollet discusses Blier's association of the female genitalia with 'dirt, and putrefaction' (Rollet 1994: 237–8). An example of this is the scene early in *Les Valseuses* where Jean-Claude and Pierrot touch Marie-Ange's pubic hair with the words 'toucher quelque chose de sale, ça porte chance. C'est comme marcher dans la merde'. ('It's good to touch something dirty for luck. It's like walking in shit.')

The instances cited above indeed appear to lend themselves to a conventionally problematic reading of the presence and actions of women in film, as defined by feminist theorists: in Blier's work, men are unambiguously the perpetrators of the action, with women inevitably perceived as the victims of the action, targets who are defeated by brute force, material concerns, or their own unchecked and uncontrollable sexual desire, and frequently by a combination of all three. With the exception of *Calmos*, the male is a virile, sexually aggressive presence, exerting near-total physical and narrative control over the the female subject. He is witty, charismatic and invites our engagement as spectators, whereas she is more typically sexually submissive and emotionally passive, and this positioning of the female subject in a consenting role with regard to the male therefore works, on a superficial level at least, to reinforce entrenched social and cultural views of women as weak or inferior sexual objects. The classic Oedipal narrative is worked out as the female subject assumes the role of the threatening passive object upon which the male protagonist must act if he is to complete his trajectory within the conventions of patriarchy. In a classic reading of these patterns, Blier's male appears to overcome the threat posed by the female's sexual difference by fetishising her body and her sexual function, and forcing her to comply with his dominant subjectivity, which in turn reinforces the stability and naturalness of the patriarchal order. Thus, Blier's approach does seem consistent with miso-gynistic tendencies which translate fear and hatred of the female mind, body and sexuality into forms which are less threatening, and which privilege the one who fears over the feared object.

This outwardly reductive pattern of male–female relationships, where male characters tend to control the action, dialogue and narrative development of the films, extends to Blier's wider dramatic construction. Women are not, on the whole, centrally placed in the films, and when they are, as in *Merci la vie, Un deux trois soleil* and *Mon homme*, powerful characteristics are ascribed to them which arguably work against any empowering image of strong womanhood. In the opening scenes of the first of these two female-centred films, the woman is either brutalised or infantilised, weakening from the outset the spectator's identification with her, regardless of how the male subject is positioned thereafter: in *Merci la vie* we witness, *in medias res*, a brutal physical attack on Joëlle; in *Un deux trois soleil*, we first see Victorine in extreme close shot, being fed a sloppy *tartine* by her mother. Similarly, in *Mon homme*, the gestural defiance, verbal aggressivity and eventual coercion of a woman into prostitution force an immediate critical distance between the spectator and the character of Marie. In the earlier films, the largely passive performance style of Marie-Ange (*Les Valseuses*), Solange (*Préparez vos mouchoirs*), Donatienne (*Notre histoire*) and Florence (*Trop belle pour toi*) creates a difficulty of identification for the female subject: her latent sympathy for Blier's women victims is frustrated, and she suffers an alienation which she is powerless to counter.

This general pattern in Blier's films of active males dominating a secondary female presence in the narrative, is further reinforced in the typical outnumbering of female characters by males. This is seen in the trios of two men–one woman present in *Les Valseuses*, *Préparez vos mouchoirs*, *Tenue de soirée*, and *La Femme de mon pote*, and in the almost total exclusion of women from *Buffet froid*. In *Trop belle pour toi*, where the women outnumber the men, the male is nevertheless centralised as the 'toi' of the title, and thus the character around whom the narrative action revolves. Narratives of duos are equally characterised by imbalance: in *Beau-père* by the vast difference in age between the central male and female protagonists, and in *Notre histoire* by the constancy of the central male character as opposed to the multiplicity of roles of the principal female. In all cases, the female character is less than the male, corresponding to feminist readings of the woman as 'lack' or 'absence' (Mulvey, in Mast *et al.* 1992: 746): the male characters dominate narratively, spatially, temporally and emotionally. The female characters do less than their male counterparts: they do not retaliate, are not generally proactive in the narrative, and express a general sense in the execution of their actions of not being in control of their bodies and, all too frequently, their emotions. It is possible, then, to read this passivity as expressive of a consenting indifference to the narrative that evolves and concludes wholly around the male protagonists. Elsewhere, the animation of the characters played by Anouk Grinberg, which is such a striking feature of *Merci la vie, Un deux trois soleil* and *Mon homme*, is grotesque rather than redeeming: it has a maniacal, uncontrolled quality quite unlike anything expressed by the range of male characters across the corpus of films. Even a wild, menacing male character like Bob in *Tenue de soirée* is characterised by physical restraint and paced, almost poetic speech, with an effect that is seductive rather than alienating. The grotesque is thus much more disturbing when located in the female rather than the male, as this explicitly contradicts established codes about attractiveness and decorum in female cinematic representation.

However, Blier has nevertheless enjoyed considerable commercial success in France over the last twenty years, a success which inevitably includes a large female spectatorship. He has also worked with an impressive range of female actors, many of whom have returned to work with him again and again.[4] Although it would be disingenuous not to take account of employment patterns in a traditionally precarious industry, there is nevertheless clearly an attraction to working with Blier to which these women respond. Indeed, Miou-Miou, whom one critic writing about *Les Valseuses* described as: 'pauvre Miou-Miou si charmante au café-théâtre et qui méritait un meilleur sort', ('Poor Miou-Miou. She was so charming in the café-théâtre, and she deserved better than this' (Domarchi 1974: 66)) responded to a question on misogyny in *Tenue de soirée* as follows

> Qu'est-ce qu'un film misogyne? En ce moment [1986], on voit un tas de films avec des hommes: *Les Ripoux, Marche à l'ombre, Les Spécialistes, Trois Hommes et un couffin, Rambo* et tout le saint frusquin. Bertrand, lui, écrit des rôles pour les femmes, des rôles magnifiques. Ce serait maso de dire qu'il est miso. (Alion 1986: 58)[5]

4 In 1992, Josiane Balasko came to the French Film Festival at Glasgow Film Theatre, and responded to a question I put to her about Blier. She was categorical in her view that Blier was the director she most enjoyed working with because he created genuinely unusual and challenging roles for women.

5 'What is a misogynistic film anyway? At the moment [1986] all you see are films with men in them: *Les Ripoux, Marche à l'ombre, Les Spécialistes, Trois Hommes et un couffin, Rambo* and that kind of thing. Bertrand at least creates parts for women, terrific parts. To call him a misogynist would simply be masochistic.'

Grinberg's assertion that 'je ne suis pas une fille qui se laisse faire' ('I'm not the kind of girl you can push around' (France Culture 1995)) along with Miou-Miou's admonition that 'les comédiens ne sont pas de pauvres choses qui subissent' ('actors aren't poor things who can't think for themselves' (Alion 1986: 58)) reiterates this point, underlining the choice that actors of their calibre make when selecting roles and working with prominent directors.

Far from hating women, as the term misogyny suggests, an accusation that Blier himself vehemently denies, it can be argued that in his exploration of modern masculinity in crisis, Blier expresses an understanding of, and a sympathy with, the condition of the liberated female in what is, at least outwardly, still a man's world. Indeed, the elements of misogynistic discourse outlined above, serve in the films to actively expose misogyny as an entrenched condition of modern male–female relationships, exploring it visibly in a way that is unusual in male-authored cinema. Furthermore, as we shall see, the expression and representation of misogyny as some kind of belief system on the part of the *auteur* is countered not only by processes of inversion and reversal in the conventional key narrative structures of image and positioning – that is to say by rendering the image and position of the female subject different from what might be termed the norm – but by a process of subversion in performance, a process of displacement of order which feeds into the images and positioning of all the characters of the narrative, not just the females. In this way, Blier's view of the social formation can be seen, like Bakhtin's, to be essentially marginocentric, acknowledging the potential, and indeed the necessity, of locating agency within the traditionally marginal voices of society, while at the same time subverting the hierarchies of conventional cinematic representation as they relate to codes of gender construction. In terms of dramatic action, this approach is entirely consistent with the practices of popular carnivalesque expression.

Essentially, Blier's ambiguous construction of female representation mounts a series of explicit challenges to cinematic conventions, and these are brought together in a subversive approach to what Stam has termed the 'hegemony of the visible' (Stam 1992: 159). Codes of attractiveness, emotional response, and female corporeality are all explored and subverted in Blier's construction, and, consistent with the need to retain the festive dimension of images, the comic potential of the female body in relation to both the male body, and the wider community, is highlighted. What emerges in this representation is that woman is constructed, as Bakhtin has suggested, very positively, as embodying the mutually complementary, and socially imperative qualities of debasement and regeneration. She is constructed not as the object of travesty, as a superficial reading of the films might suggest, but rather as the vehicle for travesty, the one who undoes the 'specific codes of cultural coherence' (Butler 1990: 131) which underpin a patriarchal ordering of social and cinematic organisation. Woman in Blier's films, as in the carnival tradition, is an essentially transgressive figure, whose powerful, regenerative presence acts as a constant check to an otherwise dominant phallocentric discourse. Her presence is disturbing to patriarchal society, insofar as her 'unfinished body' represents both the destruction of imposed social boundaries and taboos, and the ultimate permeability of the human character. Moreover, in cinematic terms, her consistently ambiguous narrative function and unconventional image also pose a threat to the established gender hierarchy with which spectators are familiar.

The codes of attractiveness and unattractiveness that inform all construction of female image in mainstream commercial cinema are dealt with subversively by Blier, with his individual female subjects embodying simultaneously a range of qualities indicative of conventional notions of beauty, and a range of equally effective qualities which complicate the perception of this beauty, and its consequent desirability. Marie-Ange in *Les Valseuses* is in many respects a prototype for the female subjects that follow in the later films insofar as the sexual appetite and ability of the character are revealed to be at odds with the externally coded view we are invited to take of her (blond, mini skirt, uninhibited nudity). She displays outward qualities of being sexy, but her behaviour and demeanour are not erotically coded for either the male protagonist or the spectator, since the actual performance of her sexuality conflicts with the image provided by the constructing elements; she is unresponsive to sexual stimulation by Jean-Claude and Pierrot, and takes no determining role in building a sexual relationship with them. Again, Florence in *Trop belle pour toi* is advanced as an example of classic beauty, embodying classically feminine qualities of elegance, sophistication and refinement, but the character's expression of these suggests sterile and aloof womanhood, rather than the complementary warmth conventionally associated with desirable femininity. Florence is thus not cast as an erotic presence in the narrative, whereas the plump, unrefined Colette is cast as the object of the male protagonist's sexual desire. This pattern of interplay in female actors between external features, spectatorial expectations created by these, and the more expressive psychological dimension of the characters is repeated throughout Blier's films, and is one of the most innovative and challenging aspects of his work.

In Blier's work, therefore, female roles are extremely complex, problematising both the female psyche, and also, and as importantly, given the visual impact of cinematic representation, the female physique. Blier's characteristic representation of women refuses the commonplace simplicity and covert eroticism of conventional cinematic portrayals of the female, the representation identified by Laura Mulvey: Blier's actresses do not easily connote what Mulvey has termed 'to-be-looked-at-ness', that is to say, they do not have an appearance which is 'coded for strong visual and erotic impact' (Mulvey, in Mast *et al.* 1992: 750). In Blier's system of images, the visual is not straightforwardly equated with the erotic, and Blier actively works against the cinematic tenet that the female subject is always and necessarily an erotic subject, simply by virtue of being female; the female in Blier's films is neither always desirous, nor indeed is she always desirable. Thus the 'significant corporeality' (Butler 1990: 136), which usually expresses cinematic gender, is disrupted by Blier's mode of representation, resulting in a cinematically unconventional denial of bodily eroticism. As Stam has noted, this denial has been identified by Bakhtin as a fundamentally carnivalesque trope

> Bakhtin's view of the body is democratic and anti-hierarchical ... By calling attention to the paradoxical attractiveness of the grotesque body, Bakhtin rejects what might be called the 'fascism of beauty', the construction of an ideal type or language of beauty in relation to which other types are seen as inferior 'dialectical' variations. (Stam 1992: 159)

Like the strong, successful – but all too rare – women of classic Hollywood cinema, Blier's females, like those identified by Molly Haskell, 'defy emotional gravity, ... go against the grain of prevailing notions about the female sex' (Haskell 1974: 4). Indeed, an immediate subversion of both narrative and gender orders is implicit in their narrative presence as remarkable women, that is women to whom we and the diegetic observers are drawn because of their construction as 'other'. In a cinema dominated by young beautiful appendages to desirable men, a cinema peopled, as Ginette Vincendeau has suggested, by 'fathers and daughters' (Vincendeau 1992: 14), Blier releases women from the constraints of the conventionally beautiful cinematic female. Women in his films are allowed an image which is highly uncommon in French cinema, where the female lead is almost invariably the epitome of ever-more youthful French glamour and chic. An actress with an unconventional physique, like Josiane Balasko for example, has generally only found leading lady success in satirical social comedies like *Les Hommes préfèrent les grosses*, and *Ma Vie est un enfer*, which, as their titles suggest, deal with the difficulties of social integration for those who have an uncommon image,[6] or more recently *Gazon maudit*, in which Balasko plays a woman who challenges assumptions about gender, without actually challenging the stereotype to which mainstream commercial

6 This is a pattern which is repeated elsewhere in popular culture. The work of the American comedienne Roseanne Barr, for example, focuses on emphasising difference rather than challenging assumptions about the dominant view. The appeal to disproportion and deformity as an opportunity for laughter and satire on which both Roseanne and Balasko's brand of comedy depends is a longstanding feature of the popular comic tradition, but it is unusual to see women – or indeed male – artists develop this beyond expressly comic genres.

cinema traditionally subscribes.[7] This is equally the case for unconventional-looking male actors like Michel Blanc, or Gérard Jugnot, from the same background as Balasko, and who have also worked with Blier; but this transition seems to have proved less problematic for men. To suggest that such a woman as Colette might be attractive, especially when in competition with no less an icon than Carole Bouquet, Buñuel's 'obscure object of desire' works against the spectator's conditioning with regard to female representation, and thereby challenges the spectator's expectations about the equation 'attractiveness equals desirability'. *Tenue de soirée* explores a similar idea: in an ironic reversal of the Cinderella syndrome the down-at-heel, drab Monique, even when transformed into a conventionally (cinematically) beautiful female in the course of the film, is ultimately no more desirable to the male she desires. He, of course, desires Antoine (Blanc), a man without conventional qualities of male attractiveness. Attractiveness then, for Blier's female actors, is set at a level beyond that which is outwardly visible, paralleling a treatment which is accorded to the males and has been commented on at length elsewhere.[8] Thus, the portrayal of both sexes is equally creative and challenging: the balanced emphatic countering of conventional readings of these images is striking in the way in which it engages with wider issues of gender portrayal,[9] and with the subversive ethos of gender representation in traditional popular culture.

Blier also inverts the conventional place of the female in the narrative. In traditional theatre and film, the female lead is frequently relegated to a secondary level, providing often no more than the sex interest of the story, or the romantic or love interest in more classic examples. She is either this, or else overly strong, distinctive for her unusual qualities of strength – a heroine –

---

7 It is of note that these films were all either written or directed (or both) by Balasko, who has largely created her own opportunities for exposure in French cinema. *Trop belle pour toi* was her first foray into a non-comic mode, and into a project in which she herself had not had authorial input.

8 See in particular Forbes (1992: 72–88).

9 See, for example, Butler (1990, 1993), and Judith Lorber (1994).

presented usually as having qualities more commonly associated with male characters (strength, courage, emotional control), and she thus takes the male place in the narrative action. In Blier's films, women are more ambiguously presented, as is the case in *Les Valseuses*: although Marie-Ange's character is secondary to that of the two males in the narrative, her sexuality is central rather than marginal to the action. Although this example may recall conventional narrative structures of the type set out in the introduction to this discussion, the narrative is not handled in such a way that the leading roles revert unproblematically to the males. In other words, Marie-Ange's frigidity does not serve only to recentre narrative interest on the heroes and how they resolve the enigma. Crucially, the enigma posed by the woman's presence (her sexuality) remains incomprehensible to them throughout the narrative, and the resolution of this narrative dilemma is under the control and the private gaze of the female protagonist: her orgasm takes place on her own terms, away from their, and the spectator's, gaze. The spectacle is refused to both parties as the shutters to the room where this will take place are closed by Marie-Ange, and she creates a private non-filmic space which she determines and defines. In this way, the carnivalesque comic potential of the body out of control – in a state of orgasm – and the incomprehension of the male characters before this elemental and creative force, is comically rendered without recourse to an overly codified representation.

The portrayal of woman in film is, as Mulvey, Haskell and others have pointed out, most frequently encoded as pleasurable. In Mulvey's view, the woman in film is an 'icon, displayed for the gaze and enjoyment of men, the active controllers of the look' (Mulvey, in Mast *et al.* 1992: 753). Her transformation into a fetishised object (in other words her over-valuation as a 'beautiful' figure) functions to make her a reassuring rather than a dangerous presence for the male protagonist. It follows then that naked, she is all the more erotic a spectacle, there for us, like the protagonist, to take pleasure in, and as such constitutes even less of a threat to all parties. Blier's frequent positioning of the woman as naked and in view of the male gaze therefore appears to suggest that he actively seeks to appeal to this particular view of her. Yet, despite the frequent recurrence of images of female nudity in Blier's work, this is rarely presented as spectacle. This has led to some confusion about Blier's intentions: there is so much visible sexuality, yet so little that is constructed according to conventional codes of erotic pleasure. The camera, for example, is rarely used to fragment the woman's body, and guide the spectator's eye around the parts of the body in the voyeuristic way common to much mainstream commercial cinema:[10] the image of the whole rather than the part is what dominates the screen in Blier's work, creating an unusual and therefore frequently disturbing perspective for the spectator.

This technique has a subversive effect on narrative construction. For example, in a scene from *Préparez vos mouchoirs*, in the implied aftermath of love-making with Stéphane, as he waxes lyrical about fate, destiny and love to a background soundtrack of Mozart, Solange sits naked, knitting. She is indifferent to the intense emotion that Stéphane expresses, an emotion and depth of feeling which is more commonly associated with the female than the male in romantic conventions; as Judith Lorber has pointed out, 'Women in Western cultural productions have represented not only men's sexual desires but also the extravagant emotions the hero cannot express without losing his manliness' (Lorber 1994: 102). Thus, Solange's sheer obliviousness to Stéphane's emotional expression, and her investing of importance in a much more banal activity, constitutes a subtle reversal of the male–female roles, one that has a clear comic function which favours the female. There is an undisguised transference of cinematised female traits (sentimentality, tenderness, excessive emotion) to the male protagonist and an ironic highlighting of a series of romantic conventions which privileges, where generally it would undermine, the woman's identity in the narrative. And although Solange is naked throughout the scene, it is precisely

10 The fragmentation of the body is a convention of pornography, and of erotic codifying. See for example the work of Andrea Dworkin, and in particular Dworkin (1981) *Pornography: Men Possessing Women*, New York, Women's Press.

because her nudity is not invested with emotion or a 'redeeming eroticism' that the spectator is unable to be stimulated or take substantial pleasure from this portrayal of her body. There is in fact a subtle negation of Mulvey's thesis about 'to-be-looked-at-ness' operating here, with the intellectual and comic appeal deriving from other elements in the scene.[11]

In this film, Yves Alion accused Blier of misogyny, and of pandering to too conventional an interpretation of the woman's place in film: 'dommage que Blier ne propose pas une vision des rôles respectifs de l'homme et de la femme moins entachée de conventions' ('what a shame that Blier doesn't try to give a less clichéd interpretation of male and female roles' (Alion 1978: 58)). But where the approach to the female presence as identified by Mulvey sees that 'visual presence tends to work against the development of a story line, to freeze the flow of the action in moments of erotic contemplation' (Mulvey, in *Mast et al.* 1992: 750), Blier's approach, precisely by focusing on an apparent, or superficial, sexual spectacle, allows the woman to be something different. Solange's unselfconsciousness frees her from the acknowledgement, or guilt, of serving as an object of desire, and she herself negates the desire she is expected to inspire; her expression of her sexuality is very crucially her own statement, and not one determined or controlled by the male agent. The nakedness of the woman does not therefore force the spectator to hesitate and contemplate her erotic presence in the film, but rather the very lack of inhibition that she has with regard to her own nakedness communicates a powerful transcendence of her physical aspect. Although the camera hides very little from us, and even circles round to take in the woman's body visually, it is very difficult to gauge the level of pleasure the spectator might

11 This scene is even more revealing when read in the context of Stam's discussion of what Ruby Rich has designated 'Medusan' feminist films, a term taken from Cixous's 'Laugh of the Medusa' 'where the French theorist celebrates the potential of feminist texts to "blow up the law, to break up 'the truth' with laughter"'. Although Blier's film can in no way be considered a 'feminist text', the same directing of 'satirical laughter against what Luce Irigaray calls ' "l'esprit du sérieux" of phallocentrism', is achieved in this scene and others (Stam 1992: 120–1).

obtain from the image alone. This casualness with regard to their bodies, clothed or otherwise, is characteristic of Blier's female actors and is repeated throughout his work, from the model in *Hitler, connais pas!*, to Miou-Miou early in *Les Valseuses*, to Grinberg in *Merci la vie, Un deux trois soleil* and *Mon homme*. It is significant in that in Blier's films, the performance of lack of inhibition is not confined to one gender category, but rather the expression of this extends to both male and female characters, recalling in general narrative terms the 'free interplay between the body and the world' (Stam 1992: 157), which is characteristic of the carnival rites.

The passivity, lack of emotional depth and general unresponsiveness of the female subjects in Blier's work has another subversive function at the level of performance. The refusal to participate in, encourage or even acknowledge the actions of the males creates a situation whereby the female characters do not legitimise in any way the violence or sexual acts that are perpetrated upon them. Blier refuses to let the legitimising process outlined by Joan Smith in her book *Misogynies* take place: the female in his work has these things done to her *because* she has no choice, leaving the male characters (and the spectator) to question their own actions and their role in an undisguised misogynistic process. Indeed, the three-in-the-bed sex scene where Jean-Claude and Pierrot first become aware of Marie-Ange's inability to experience sexual arousal does not show the female as the butt of the joke, as a misogynist reading would have it, but rather satirises the male expectation that the woman will enjoy what is being done to her regardless of the men's lack of emotional and physical investment. The two male characters expect the female to react in accordance with their expectations, gleaned not so much from experience as from lack of it. For them, she should be moaning, have her eyes half-closed in pleasure, be perspiring, glowing; instead, she displays no physical or emotional reaction whatsoever to their efforts, leaving them confused and frustrated. In this way, she refuses to acknowledge the social taboos that institute and maintain the boundaries of the female body as conventionally represented by the cinema, performing an inherently transgressive act, both with regard to her male counterparts, and to the spectating audience. Although not very conventionally, then, some rights are restored to the woman: we understand that it is the male characters who are inadequate, and who have been conditioned to have certain expectations about female sexuality: it is from them, not the woman, that the spectator is invited to take his or her distance. As indicated above, when Marie-Ange does experience sexual fulfilment, neither the viewer nor the two protagonists actually see the event – it is private – and the male characters' inadequacy as the irresistible sex machines they believe themselves to be is all the more risible: against a highly comic tableau of idyllic river scenes and gushing water, the mechanical parallel actions of Jean-Claude and Pierrot highlight their incomprehension and ultimate exclusion from the processes of narrative resolution.

Coercive action against women takes place across the range of films, and, compounded by the passivity outlined above, is generally perceived as something which happens to the woman, something outwith her control, something which has a further important reductive effect on her female identity. This, however, is not always the case, and examination of one of the most controversial examples from the films will illustrate how, in Blier's work, a process of reversal of spectatorial expectation takes place which allows the woman to act and comment on the narrative events that encompass her. The example, from *Les Valseuses*, is a disturbing scene, which has almost unanimously been read as expressive of a misogynistic abuse of male power. Brigitte Fossey plays a nursing mother, travelling in a train, who, while feeding her baby, is accosted by the two male aggressors Jean-Claude and Pierrot. This is intended by the male characters to be a very erotic episode: their intention is to become sexually aroused so that Pierrot can prove to himself that he is still virile, but this quite unambiguously backfires on them, and the eroticism which emerges is, paradoxically for them and the spectator, located within and for the female subject. After considerable resistance, the character played by Fossey consents to allow Pierrot to suck at her breast in return for money proffered by Jean-Claude. As the action of the scene advances, the mother clearly begins to experience a sexual pleasure that surpasses the arousal of the men. Yet, at the same time she continues to look directly at her aggressors, refusing to see them as such, and challenging them to make sense of her reactions. In this way, the female character rejects the abuse of male power that they seek to enact on her, and displaces the centre of narrative attention, against the narrative agents, from the male to the female.

In terms of a reading of this image in the context of popular expressive forms, it is carnivalesque on a number of levels: in its emphasis on physicality, sexual potency and regeneration, in its exploration of tropes of usurpation, and in its achievement of a liberation of energies where usually they would remain constrained, or even explicitly repressed by the dominant codes of social organisation. There is initially an iconoclastic assault on the sacred image of the madonna and child, combined with an exploration of the *puer-senex* trope, as the man assumes the place and function of the child in the narrative action. Second, there is a cultural subversion of the conventions of both social and sexual behaviour: the exchange of money in return for sexual favours from the maternal body constitutes a debasement of the codes of both commercial, but principally familial exchange. Finally, there is an apparent validation of the classic madonna–whore image, so common to cinematic representation, a validation which is undermined by the camera's relentless focus on male impotence, both physical and emotional. These subversive attacks on the iconography and manners of social convention, focused as they are on the functions of nurturing and regeneration, are entirely typical of the carnival which, as Stam makes clear

> operates a perpetual decanonization. Rather than high art's sublimation, we are given a strategy of reduction and degradation, which uses obscenity, scatology, burlesque and caricature to turn upside down all the forms and values by which, in Pierre Bourdieu's words, 'the dominant groups project and recognize their sublimity'. (Stam 1992: 110)

Moreover, a deeper level of subversion operates with regard to the gendered context of the action in focus, demolishing the social taboos which, as Butler has suggested, 'institute and maintain the boundaries of the body ... as the limits of the socially *hegemonic*' (Butler 1990: 131). Here, the female refuses to be complicit in the intended process of her own subordination, precisely by her assumption of an active role in the reversal of the representational codes of unequal gender relationships.

Misogyny, according to Joan Smith's various analyses does not acknowledge that the female psyche is active, or that women can control their own sexuality. For Blier to demonstrate, then, that the woman has a choice about her sexual nature, and that this can operate, as the above example makes clear, outside societal taboos about the female body, seems to express the very opposite of a misogynistic viewpoint. To show the woman experiencing pleasure by switching from one act to another – from nurturing to a sexual situation – seems rather to allow what a feminist interpretation would hold true, that there are no easy divisions: the woman lives with both aspects of her femaleness. What is disturbing and problematic about this scene in *Les Valseuses* is the witnessing of the action itself, combined with the awareness on the part of the spectator that the woman chooses to participate on her own terms and derive pleasure from the experience; no attempt is made to disguise in performance or *mise-en-scène* the multiple or plural nature of the female body, and the certainty about this in the woman's own mind, allowing Blier to bring together two funda-mental and culturally exclusive aspects of the female body in a way that defies and defeats male control. This corresponds not only to a feminist reading of female sexuality, but also to the reading of sexuality within the popular festive tradition which 'always exists in relation – in relation to the general existence of the body, in relation to other persons, and in relation to the "labouring life of the social whole"' (Stam 1992: 161).

As in the carnivalesque popular tradition, taboos on women are traditionally associated with their physical and sexual nature, and Blier's subversion of the conventional images of female corpore-ality and behaviour constitutes a refusal to respect and therefore to perpetuate accepted taboos. Throughout his films, Blier explores and exposes moral and aesthetic taboos by concentrating on rather banal commonplaces of sexual fantasy (sex on demand, multiple or willing sexual partners, sex with strangers) while refusing the eroticism aimed at the male spectator with which these images have traditionally been invested. This process of subversion has a major narrative consequence: the male subject is displaced as the centre of meaning in the narrative at these times, a displacement which informs the overall narrative structure of the individual films, and by extension Blier's whole corpus of work. Indeed, Blier's final scenes, to which we might look for any authorial message to take away with us, typically depict the male characters in a state of 'exclusion, failure and decrepitude' (King 1996: 9) whereas the female characters are frequently depicted in a very positive light: Solange is finally pregnant and smiling, Marie-Ange is at ease with herself and with her two companions, and is instrumental in introducing another young woman to sexual pleasure (crucially transmitting her own experience, not that of the males, to another woman). In *Tenue de soirée* the male characters are transformed by costume and fantasy into 'women', and in *Trop belle pour toi* both women abandon the man, who is left railing at the camera–spectator. What this clearly seems to indicate is that the endings of Blier's films convey empowerment and progress, a triumph of the regenerative and productive female spirit over the male, and a degree of certainty that the female, rather than the male, in fact constitutes the narrative power base of the films.

It is therefore via a system of processes of inversion in performance and *mise-en-scène* that Blier effectively subverts the key narrative structures that support an initial misogynistic reading of his work. Blier's inversions, which take as their starting point the filmic norms of commercial narrative cinema, allow for narrative subversion on a scale that is unusual in mainstream cinema, and which is all the more subversive for taking place within the identified parameters of misogynistic discourse. The parodic imitation of gendered action and identities which Blier operates has an important function within the context of modes of gender subversion. As Butler has pointed out

> Parodic proliferation deprives hegemonic culture and its critics of the claim to naturalized or essentialist gender identities. Although the gender meanings taken up in these parodic styles are clearly part of a hegemonic, misogynist culture, they are nevertheless denaturalized and mobilized through their parodic recontextualization. (Butler 1990: 138)

Blier's achievement of the denaturalising and mobilising of gender meanings in his films accords with the wider approach to parodic performance which characterises popular dramatic expression. In Stam's words

> Parody ... is the privileged mode of artistic carnivalization. By appropriating an existing discourse but introducing into it an orientation oblique or even diametrically opposed to that of the original, parody ... is especially well suited to the needs of oppositional culture, precisely because it deploys the force of the dominant discourse against itself. (Stam 1992: 173)

It is in this process of narrative subversion that Blier's innovation with regard to female representation lies: far from perpetrating an unchallenging and ideologically conservative view of the female in terms of image and position, Blier's innovative and challenging patterns of gender subversion in performance directly engage with traditions of representation which valorise and privilege the female presence.

If, as Molly Haskell suggests, a woman, in cinema as in society is 'supposedly most herself in the throes of emotion (the love of a man or a child)' (Haskell 1974: 4) then Blier's experiment with the fine balance of conventional female cinematic roles is a highly innovative and progressive one. He empowers the female subject by liberating her not only from conventional patterns of representation, but also from the suffocating libertarianism that was such a commonplace of films, particularly French films, of the post-sexual revolution. Marie-Ange and Solange's apparent frigidity can be alternatively read as an expression of their fatigue or *ennui* at the cultural and sexual expectations of them both as women and as modes of representation, as well as of that very emotional apathy that Haskell sees as the lot of the cinematic female in the early 1970s, the woman who has been so many (but frequently the same) things to so many men (mother, mistress, saint, whore, enigma, lover) that she has arrived 'anaesthetized, at an emotional and cultural "stasis", a death' (Haskell 1974: 41).[12] For a male director to explore this, specifically in performance, and to anticipate so much of what is of concern to feminist commentators may surely be argued to be progressive? What Blier effectively achieves in his work is in fact a forceful denial of the 'social fiction' described by Judith Butler, which says that woman is a 'sedimentation of gender norms' fixed in her corporeal style (Butler 1990: 140), and to which codes of female representation have long been bound. It is precisely through the performance of 'subversive bodily acts' (Butler 1990: 79–141) in Blier's work that female identity achieves a liberating instability, or permeability which accords with the type of representation we find in the popular tradition. This overt subversion of the hierarchy of patriarchal authority through processes of de-eroticisation and conflation of gender boundaries is, as Robert Stam has pointed out, intensely carnivalesque

> Against a patriarchal ideology of innate difference, Bakhtin implicitly exalts the blurring and shifting of gender distinctions, a release from the burden of socially imposed sex roles. Bakhtin lauds the androgynous body of carnival representation. (Stam 1992: 163)

Ultimately, then, the challenge to a dominant phallocentricity, expressed through the utopian view that the female, like the male, can be 'other', is central to, and inherently positive within, Blier's dramatic exploration of popular forms.

---

12 It is interesting to note that *Les Valseuses* coincided with the period of publication of the Haskell text, and slightly pre-dated Mulvey.

References

Alion, Yves (1978), 'Préparez vos mouchoirs', *Ecran* 66, February, 58.

Alion, Yves (1986), 'Entretien avec Miou-Miou: des *Valseuses* à *Tenue de soirée*', *Revue du cinéma* 417, June, 58.

Anzalone, John (1990), *French Review* 63, 567–8.

Bakhtin, Mikhail (1984), *Rabelais and his World* (trans. Hélène Iswolsky), Bloomington, Indiana University Press.

Butler, Judith (1990), *Gender Trouble: Feminism and the Subversion of Identity*, London, Routledge.

Butler, Judith (1993), *Bodies that Matter: On the Discursive Limits of 'Sex'*, London, Routledge.

Domarchi, Jean (1974), 'Les Valseuses', *Ecran* 25, May, 66.

Dworkin, Andrea (1981), *Pornography: Men Possessing Women*, New York, Women's Press.

Forbes, Jill (1992), *The Cinema in France: After the New Wave*, London, Macmillan.

France Culture (1995), 'Le bon plaisir de Bertrand Blier', broadcast 18 February 1995.

Harris, Sue (1996), 'Image, Position, Performance: Misogyny and the Female Subject in the Films of Bertrand Blier', in Sue Harris and Russell S. King (1996), *Bertrand Blier and Misogyny, Stirling French Publications* 4, 12–25.

Haskell, Molly (1974), *From Reverence to Rape: the Treatment of Women in the Movies*, New York, Holt, Rinehart & Winston.

King, Russell S. (1996) 'Bertrand Blier's Men Behaving Badly: the Question of Misogyny', in Sue Harris and Russell S. King (1996), *Bertrand Blier and Misogyny, Stirling French Publications* 4, 1–11.

Lorber, Judith (1994) *Paradoxes of Gender*, New York, Yale University Press.

Mulvey, Laura (1975) 'Visual Pleasure and the Narrative Cinema', originally published in *Screen* 16:3, autumn 1975, reproduced in Gerald Mast, Marshall Cohen and Leo Braudy (eds) (1992), *Film Theory and Criticism: Introductory Readings* (4th edn), New York and Oxford, Oxford University Press.

Rollet, Brigitte (1994) 'The Man who Disliked Women': Blier – Misogynist or 'Gynophobe'? (trans. Renate Gunther), in Renate Gunther and Jan Windebank (eds), *Violence and Conflict in Modern French Culture*, Sheffield, Sheffield Academic Press.

Smith, Joan (1989) *Misogynies*, London, Faber & Faber.

Stam, Robert (1992) *Subversive Pleasures: Bakhtin, Cultural Criticism and Film*, Baltimore, Johns Hopkins University Press.

Vincendeau, Ginette (1992) 'The Fathers and Daughters of French Cinema', *Sight and Sound*, March 14–17.

5

A farewell to arms:
Blier's 'second career'

At the time of the release of *Un deux trois soleil* in 1994, Blier announced in an interview that 'Je suis entré dans ma deuxième carrière. Sur ces deux derniers films je me suis davantage impliqué en tant qu'individu' ('I've begun my second career. I've invested more of myself in these last two films' (*Merci la vie* and *Un deux trois soleil*) (Vecchi 1993: 25–6)). But, in some ways, the transition indicated by the director is not immediately obvious to the viewer: theme and style in *Merci la vie* and *Un deux trois soleil*, together with *Mon homme*, Blier's most recent film, are unambiguously 'du Blier', as are the ensemble-type comic performances. Indeed, what might usefully be regarded as a trilogy of films clearly looks back to Blier's earlier work through a combination of, on the one hand, depictions of sexuality and excess, and ludic visual and verbal humour typical of the comic films, and on the other, the intimate psychological tone and abstract or digressive narrative forms of the films predominantly of the 1980s. The dramatic and structural features of inversion and subversion established by Blier in his earlier work are crucial to the narrative construction of these films, as is the expression of a utopian urge through a thematic exploration of the nature and function of community, and male–female relations. The carnivalesque motif is extended in these films, which emphasise thematically and dramatically moments of death and revival (symbolic in *Merci la vie* and *Mon homme*; literal in *Un deux trois soleil*), and an intrinsic link is made in all three films between sex and death, *eros* and *thanatos*, and the cyclical nature of both film-making and life. Furthermore, the films extend the dramatic conception of the earlier work through a continued emphasis on the depiction of cultures of marginality and, more importantly, through a system of self-referentiality, which posits the earlier films as intertext. It becomes clear very early in the trilogy that Blier is deliberately reworking character types and dramatic configurations, through a process of 'quotation' of previous characters and key images and scenes.

There is, however, a great deal of evidence to support Blier's claim that these films mark a new stage in his work. The most striking indication of a distance between these films and those that pre-date them is in the deployment of a series of central female protagonists, whose characterisation challenges the modes of representation previously established in Blier's work. It is the case that this ground had already been tested in *Trop belle pour toi* in 1989, but *Merci la vie* nevertheless marks a venture into new female territory for Blier: this is signalled from the first scene in which Joëlle appears in that most classic example of female attire, a bridal dress, recalling the passive Florence of *Trop belle pour toi*. She is immediately attacked by 'un mec qui corrige' ('a bloke who likes to use his fists'), and is left railing an ironic 'merci la vie' ('thanks a lot, life') at the deserted street in which he leaves her lying. We appear for all the world to be on familiar Blierian ground: the 'début coup de poing' ('in your face opening scene' (Pagnon 1991: 26–7)), the aggressed female victim, the incongruous characterisation expressed by costume and dialogue. The next image goes even further in confirming this sense of familiarity: the appearance of a shopping trolley into which Joëlle is unceremoniously bundled explicitly recalls the opening scene of *Les Valseuses*, the opening scene it might be said, of both Blier's and Depardieu's commercial careers.

This very potent image becomes the springboard for a series of connections which the spectator inevitably makes with characters and themes from the previous works. The trolley full of seagulls, the dishevelled Joëlle who is forced into the trolley and then sent flying by Camille (Charlotte Gainsbourg), immediately hints at a reprise of both the male buddy relationship enshrined in the

Dewaere–Depardieu duo, and at the aggressive, defiant male characterisation of many of the later films. This is confirmed for us in the scenes that follow: Joëlle is revealed as a vulgar, dynamic, predatory woman, vocal and animated and very much more ambiguous than her predecessors. Camille initially appears to be relatively passive, but she too is volatile and proactive, taking the role of willing apprentice in the adventures, sexual and otherwise, to which Joëlle introduces her. The film quickly establishes these women as errant and unstable individuals, whose construction is a complete reversal of previous modes of female characterisation. Joëlle and Camille are signalled as the Jean-Claude and Pierrot of the 1990s, a turning of tables which emphatically shifts the gender balance of Blier's subsequent work. Likewise, our first shot of Victorine in *Un deux trois soleil* presents her as a grotesque parody of the already parodic food-obsessed Paul and Albert in *Calmos*, while Marie in *Mon homme* is revealed to us in the opening scene as a menacing Bob-like seductor who quietly sits and waits to ensnare innocent passers-by.

The second major indicator of a new direction in Blier's film-making is in the increasingly complex *mise-en-scène* that we find in the three films. All are more experimental than before with regard to the temporal and spatial dimensions of the narratives, and all increase the attention to devices such as mediated narration (where characters frequently talk about self in the third person), and dramatic enactment. In *Merci la vie* the layering concept disorientates the spectator: we have a sense that we are watching a film within a film, but even this film seems to be part of another temporal and spatial mode. Here, the episodic dramatic situations of the earlier comic work are superseded by techniques of fragmentation and abstraction: movement between colour and black and white, between film and filming, between the present and the past, between fantasy and reality. The principle of rupture (stylistic and narrative) is developed to such an extent that we find the characters voicing our shared confusion: the increasingly confused Raymond Pelleveau (Michel Blanc), disorientated by the unexplained war-time activities going on around him, steps out of a scene about an attack on resistance fighters to declare: 'Je voudrais qu'on se mette bien d'accord sur l'époque dans laquelle on vit. Parce que si c'est l'époque du SIDA, alors il n'y a pas des Allemands; et si c'est l'époque des Allemands, alors il n'y a pas de SIDA. Et on baise.' ('What the hell period are we in? If there's AIDS there can't be any Nazis; and if it's the Nazi era, there's no AIDS. And we can fuck.')

As the above example shows, this series of films does in fact differ significantly from previous works in its thematic priorities. In these films, the thematic focus becomes more explicitly topical, addressing problematic aspects of specifically modern urban life, of the type familiar to more mainstream forms of French cinema. *Merci la vie* is probably the most ambitious in scope, addressing the spread of AIDS and sexually transmitted diseases, and the inhumanity of modern warfare. The two subsequent films deal with the issue of 'la fracture sociale' (the term adopted by the media to describe social breakdown in 1990s France): unemployment, immigration, life in the inner city, homelessness, prostitution, and the repressive nature of the forces of law and order are all dealt with from the point of view of the 'marginal within', the socially excluded individual upon whom this experience impacts the most. Although Blier's work has always taken the contemporary urban world as its dramatic environment, the characters we see in the trilogy are, if anything, even more firmly grounded in the social fabric of modern urban living than their hedonistic antecedents, albeit that their milieu itself is considerably more fantastic.

The endeavour, at this stage in his career, to invest his filmmaking with new stylistic and thematic energy can be understood as a response of sorts by the director to longstanding criticisms of his work. The most immediately obvious response is to the accusation of misogyny that has followed him throughout his career; here, Blier challenges his critics by putting the arguments about the location of misogynistic discourse and the nature of female representation centre stage. His abandoning of a central male pairing in favour of female protagonists, responds to criticisms that he casts women only in a passive mode as the compliant victims of male aggression, and this becomes the dramatic mechanism for not just one, but three major films. This was to some extent anticipated in the commercial and (unprecedented in Blier's career) industry success of *Trop belle pour toi*. But there the representation of women remained problematised by the very abstract qualities of the narrative, and by the unavoidable intertext (embodied in Carole Bouquet) of the woman as 'obscure object of desire' – an enigmatic, unattainable possession. In the final cycle of films, women fully inititate and conclude the narrative action, and behave in ways that are, if anything, more disturbing than those associated with males. For the first time in Blier's work, an actress is permitted to embody all the qualities of excess, deviance and transgression so characteristic – and so characteristically reassuring – of the previous male protagonists. Finally, she becomes their equal, and plays her part according to both their rules, and those of her own choosing.

Social engagement, always a feature of Blier's cinema, is here conscious and foregrounded: the view that Blier deals in triviality and titillation is difficult to sustain in a trilogy that addresses contemporary social issues on the political agenda in France in the 1990s. By extending his range of reference beyond that which supposedly appeals most to the 'anciens soixante-huitards' ('post-'68 generation'), Blier's 'new' film-making arguably seeks to engage with a wider audience than before, one that has a different composition from Blier's own peer group. Thematically, his films speak to his own generation of the limited social progress that has been made over the decades since 1968. At the same time, the departure from the mood and pace of the earlier films constitutes a direct appeal to a younger audience, and to the modes of representation with which the younger generation are familiar. Blier has indicated that part of his purpose in *Merci la vie* was to adopt new narrative strategies which corresponded to the evolution in audience skills of reception: in this case, Blier's deliberate narrative incoherence is an attempt to harness the viewing skills of a young television-literate generation of what he calls 'zappers'.[1]

1 '*Merci la vie* est un film de zappeur ... C'est ça l'idée, je zappe, tout d'un coup c'est en noir et blanc, il y a la guerre ... Les enfants font ça d'une façon magistrale, car en plus ils se passent une cassette tout en téléphonant ... C'est une gymnastique de spectateurs' ('*Merci la vie* is a channel-hopper's film. That's

Finally, Blier's renewed film-making is fascinating in as much as it clearly constitutes an open dialogue with himself and his public, and stands as a response to his own film-making practice. The films engage in a considered process of re-evaluation, of dialogue with his own previous works and dramatic techniques, and consciously exploit the earlier work as a key intertext: *Un deux trois soleil* and *Mon homme* especially are much richer when read alongside the previous films. The accumulation device that Blier exploits in performance and *mise-en-scène* is here extended to a system of images and references which directly address the spectator: this echoes the direct exchange that is part of the dramatic environment of the three diegetic worlds, wherein a dramatisation of the notion of spectatorial involvement is crucial. These films, which deal in an interrogation of the concept of illusion, maintain an exchange with the spectator at the level of overall narrative construction. In these films, Blier looks back to and renews the work of his entire career, drawing on the earlier work as inspiration, dramatic model, and as a vehicle for conclusion.

What is significant is the obvious enjoyment that Blier takes in reviewing his own work in this way. *Mon homme* emerges as a key film in Blier's career, a film which is marked by qualities of nostalgia in style, comic content, characterisation and narrative trajectory. In particular it marks an emphatic return to the comic tone and 1970s utopian expression of *Les Valseuses* (1973) and *Préparez vos mouchoirs* (1978), and the dramatic configurations build on the character groupings of the comic films: as Marie states very self-consciously in the closing moments of the film: 'je ne me suis jamais sentie aussi groupée' ('I've never felt more part of the group'). Even the title of the film hints at a nostalgic tone: the reference to Mistinguette's popular song is an explicit nod to an era, or eras, which are subject to different value systems from those in place in 1990s France. The action of the film harks back to a supposed 'golden age' of sexual behaviour, wherein sex is a

---

what it's about, you zap, and suddenly it's in black and white, it's a war film ... Kids are great at it, they can even put on a cassette and call someone at the same time. ... It's like gymnastics for viewers' (Toubiana 1991: 26–7)).

leisure pursuit like any other, enjoyed for its own sake, and without emotional dependency. In this way, the film brings Blier's career since *Les Valseuses* full circle: it is the most reminiscent, reflective and ultimately conclusive moment in his *œuvre*.

Reprise and renewal: characters, images, scenes

One important intertextual level on which the trilogy relates to the earlier work is that of characterisation. The characters played by Anouk Grinberg (Joëlle, Victorine, Marie) as stated above, recapture the qualities of insolence and brash confidence previously incarnated by key Blierian actors such as Gérard Depardieu and Miou-Miou. Grinberg is cast as the same type of disconcerting, aggressive and compelling character, verbally articulate and physically fluid, a grotesque incarnation of order (beauty) and disorder simultaneously. The corporeal, verbal and emotional sorority that she expresses with those who have featured before is explicitly signalled by Blier early in *Merci la vie*, which is the only film in which his two *acteurs fétiches* (most consistently featured artists) appear together. The first screen interaction between Grinberg and Depardieu is revealing on a number of levels: Joëlle is presented by Marc-Antoine, the doctor played by Depardieu, to a corrupt mayor as the disease carrier who will bring prosperity to the medical professionals in his consituency. The performance of the two, as Grinberg is presented to the mayor, camera and spectator by Depardieu follows the fluid circular movement of weather figures on an old-fashioned barometer: as Marc-Antoine opens a door to reveal a demure, feminine, ballerina-like figure, so he leaves by an adjoining door, ceding his established place in the Blier canon to this newcomer. As the film progresses, the sense of succession that informs their relationship beyond the diegesis is furthered in the action they perform: Marc-Antoine's role in this film is to direct and guide Joëlle's participation, to put her in difficult situations of his choosing, before abandoning her to her ambiguous inheritance.

Elsewhere, existing character type and traits are visually and thematically recalled by Blier: *Un deux trois soleil* reworks the problematic incarnations of maternity and the maternal body of *Préparez vos mouchoirs*, and extends the 'côté conte de fées' ('fairytale qualities') of Solange (Carole Laure) from the earlier film in the detached but fragile, semi-fantastic character of Victorine.[2] Marie in *Mon homme* detects new clients like Bob in *Tenue de soirée* detects 'pognon' ('dough', cash). Jeannot, Marie's pimp and ally, displays the seductive traits and physical presence of Jean-Claude (*Les Valseuses*), Raoul (*Préparez vos mouchoirs*) and Bob (*Tenue de soirée*). The adolescents who would provide Victorine with her sexual initiation are as insensitive and unknowing as those elsewhere in the canon: the observation by one participant in *Un deux trois soleil* that 'ce qu'il faut admirer chez les voyous c'est la délicatesse' ('what you've got to admire about thugs is their consideration') immediately conjures up the image of Jean-Claude and Pierrot struggling in vain to provide Marie-Ange with their own brand of sexual 'satisfaction'.

Many of the images of the trilogy are visual quotations of previous shots, and as such contribute to the mechanism of mediated narration which characterises Blier's style. In exploiting this self-referentiality, Blier provides a commentary on his own work as unfinished and organic. *Mon homme*, for example, begins with a direct visual reference to the grotesque flourish that concludes *Tenue de soirée*, that of Antoine in drag. The final shots of *Tenue de soirée* take the form of what Guy Austin has called a 'lascivious pan' (Austin 1996: 73) or an appraising sweep that takes in Antoine's body and ends with a complicit wink direct to camera. The potentially fetishising close-ups on Antoine's legs, body and face are at first erotically codified, only to be abruptly subverted by the shots of the face, which are incongruously masculine. Our view of Antoine is that of a distorted parody of the conventional *femme fatale*: the body seems perfect, but the falsity of the face disturbs the coherence of the image. *Mon homme* commences with a static

2 'J'ai choisi Carole Laure à cause de son côté bande dessinée, conte de fées, son allure un peu magique qui allait bien avec le propos du film.' ('I chose Carole Laure for her cartoon-like side, her fairytale qualities, her slightly magical ways, which suited the film well' (Haustrate 1988: 43)).

shot of an elegant arcade, at the top of which sits a figure in the same cross-legged pose as Antoine at the end of the first film. As the camera homes in on the figure, we see that this is the *femme fatale* herself, clad in the same fetishising black stockings and stiletto heels as before. Those familiar with the Blier canon, and with the Blierian character type, are immediately reassured by the image before them, and by the complicit tones of the Barry White soundtrack, an appeal to kitsch and to an easy temporal contextu-alisation: 'Hush, don't say a word ...' functions as an ironic voice-over, which echoes Antoine's wink to the spectator. As we instinctively associate, then measure the distance between the first image and the second, so we note that Antoine's lace gloves, a gesture of finery in the midst of the drab café and the bizarre situation have been transformed into the sequined *décolleté* of Marie, and the finery of the arcade. The dramatic mechanism of squabbling, which immediately precedes the shots of Antoine, is retained in *Mon homme*'s opening sequence, as are those of the character of the unlikely prostitute, the formation of an improbable alliance, and the narrative play on the words and images of *tapine/copine* ('hooker'/'pal' – a reference to streetwalking in pairs). The accosting of the passer-by (a reprise of the scene that opens *Préparez vos mouchoirs*) and the subsequent transformation of Gilberte into 'Mona' mirrors that of Antoine to Antoinette. As well as providing an example of how role-play is encoded into the dramatic mechan-isms of Blier's *mise-en-scène*, both transformations are consistent with previous examples of hierarchical and high cultural inversion. Just as Antoine's reinvention as a 'queen' strikes at the double notion of kingship (physical manhood and male authority), so Marie, the virginal incarnation of goodness, purity and maternity is here a 'pute par vocation' ('has a vocation for prostitution'), a defilement of basic cultural assumptions. Her corruption of a married woman – again an attack on traditional patriarchal authority – and her position at the foot of the Hôtel Chopin, serve to debase all notions of elegant, classic romanticism implicit in the material environment (her dress, the elaborate arcade). Marie's apparel is ultimately shown to be a costume, every bit as much as Antoine's: like him, she is not entirely what she seems to be.

As well as characters and particular images, whole scenes from Blier's earlier films provide the inspiration for dramatic incidents in the trilogy. The pursuit of Jeannot by Bérangère as he is released from prison, subtly reverses the episode from *Les Valseuses* in which Jean-Claude and Pierrot pursue Jeanne. The deserted roads are identical, the tentative following of one character by another is retained, the same sense of bewilderment is expressed by Jeanne/Jeannot. Here, the comic value of the scene is located to a large extent in the image we are given of the woman as sexual predator. In this scene, as in that in *Un deux trois soleil* where a man is aggressed by women on a train (reminiscent of the controversial nursing scene of *Les Valseuses*), comic self-referentiality conveys a sense of the male figure as 'l'arroseur arrosé' ('the biter bit').

Both *Tenue de soirée* and *Un deux trois soleil* feature Jean-Pierre Marielle (also of *Calmos*) in the role of a phlegmatic home owner who is burgled. The first scene takes place in the ethereal, elegant environment into which Bob, Antoine and Monique have intruded. In a reversal of our expectations, 'l'homme dépressif' ('the depressed man', another example of Blier's designation of character on the basis of a single dominant trait) is unperturbed at the burglary and, after extending a welcome to the burglars, seeks to engage them, against their will, in an orgy. The comic value of this scene lies in the way in which the deviance of the transgressors is transmitted to the apparently more respectable character, who is ultimately shown to be yet more dangerously subversive. But stylistically, the interest here lies in the way in which this scene constitutes a moment of aesthetic slippage within the film, giving the action an oneiric quality; the framing of the bourgeois as they descend the outer staircase, the synchronised movements of the three criminals, the attenuation of the audible apparatus all serve to convey a sense of an unreal dimension, a moment of disharmony and abstraction in an otherwise predominantly linear narrative.

In the reprise of this scene in *Un deux trois soleil*, the burglars are just as comic and inept, and Marielle again takes up the role exactly where he left it in the first film, ten years earlier. His desire to welcome rather than pursue the burglar ('ça nous fait de la visite', 'it's nice to have company') signals that this is essentially the same bored and lonely character for whom burglars are a welcome diversion. The tone of his voice, even his gestures are identical to those of the earlier version. The only difference is that he is now even more convivial and benevolent with his juvenile burglar, even though he has less to give (no Pommard and *foie gras* in this scene). The scene is a direct reworking of the first, a presentation that is first highlighted in character construction, and then intensified in the formal encoding of devices of mediated narration and storytelling. In this episode, the camera continually frames Marielle the storyteller, positioning the spectator as the knowing interlocutor. The dramatic environment is coherent from one film to the other, even to the descent of the stairs leading to the kitchen. The appeal to the burglar to stay in the guest room, and the sharing of a meal when he returns are direct quotes from the earlier film. The evolution of the character and his social conscience, however, is insufficient to prevent a tragic outcome, the death of the adult Petit Paul (who is interchangeable with the boy burglar), who is shot dead by a 'respectable' neighbour. Here there is no comic relief in the use of the gun to defuse the situation, but rather a sense of the futility and foolishness of the character played by Marielle, who understands so little of his contemporary society. The would-be utopic liaisons and transgressions of the earlier film have given way to a weary and ineffective optimism, to a crushing of all sense of natural justice, and to an abrupt dissolution of the notion of fraternity. The reprise of the same elements as before, but within a terrestrial dramatic environment which underlines the banality of 'ordinary life', emphasises the bleakness of the later vision.

This sense of disillusionment is apparent elsewhere in the final cycle, and is forcefully expressed through a development of moments of what might be termed 'cultural collision'. This type of device is much used to comic effect in the earlier films: in *Les Valseuses*, for example, the scene of the exploding car is constructed around a comic juxtaposition which is a simple but highly effective attack on cultural artefacts and aspirations. Against a backdrop of a brightly coloured field of flowers, Jean-Claude drives a stolen Morgan, an expensive British car which immediately speaks of status and wealth. The evidently rich woman whose car this is, is seen then with the bellboy of a grand hotel, looking in vain for the car that had been placed ready for her to collect. Against a series of images denoting elegance, expense, refinement and sophistication, we then cut to a scene of the car breaking down: the vulgar tirade that Jean-Claude launches against the car is entirely at odds with the dominant visual and associative context, providing an intensely comic moment, as well as an acerbic comment on the nature of bourgeois pursuits and aspirations.

By the time we reach *Merci la vie* this attack has become both more complex and more subtle. In the scene in which Joëlle is introduced to the mayor, we first associate her with beauty, grace, nature: she moves elegantly, is dressed with refinement, appears gentle. However, Marc-Antoine's verbal commentary – the anticipation of Joëlle's involvement in a scam involving promiscuity, disease and profit from the illnesses of others – provides a cruel juxtaposition with the serene image of female purity. We then cut to an image of an older woman, wearing a similar floral dress to Joëlle. In documentary style, she narrates direct-to-camera her husband's infidelity with a prostitute and the effect of his transmission of a sexual disease back to her. What has become the linking motif of flowers is then continued in the scene which follows: a man whom we assume to be the husband re-enacts the liaison, telling us that after sex with this woman 'on avait des fleurs plein la tête' ('a head full of flowers'). The episode culminates in a visual rendering of Impressionist paintings of a woman coming through the poppy fields, following the same left to right diagonal trajectory as in the works of Monet and Renoir. The verbal expression, however, again entirely negates the purity of this high cultural reference: Joëlle dreamily announces from within the image that she has slept with fathers and sons, and contaminated them all, in a way that may recall the *Dame aux camélias*. The flowers – like this woman – are deadly, and their real value will now emerge when the men inevitably suffer 'la bite en fleurs' – the burning sensation associated with the onset of a sexually transmitted disease.

By using the earlier work as an intertextual springboard, Blier conveys a sense of the evolution in attitudes that has occurred over a period of two decades of considerable social and cultural change in French society. The most recent filmic style reflects a way of life that has become both more complex and more complicated, whereas the return to tried and tested dramatic formulas hints at the circularity of the modern experience, at how what we take for social progress is simply, bleakly more of the same. It is also true, however, that Blier's trilogy is not resolutely pessimistic, and that *Mon homme* in particular is one of the most imaginatively comic of all the films that Blier has made. The deployment of hallmark features such as the free-standing comic episode format, a fast and furious dialogue, the many absurd permutations of the multiple central unit result in a film from Blier's mature career which has all the energy and spark of the early successes: *Mon homme* is as well paced as *Les Valseuses*, as witty as *Préparez vos mouchoirs*, as stylish as *Tenue de soirée*, all in all a complete comic delight. However, the difference with this film lies in the way in which characters are allowed not only to interrogate the film as it evolves, but also to express genuine emotions with regard to their participation within it: Joëlle and Jeannot can – and do – laugh at the ridiculousness of their sexual performance, are amazed at the absurdity of their transformations, and express tearful incomprehension at the sheer arbitrariness of their relationships and alliances, and the lack of control they have over their lives. It is as if Blier's familiar types have acquired a new sense of objectivity; as if they, like the director, are involved in a process of self-evaluation at the end of a long and somewhat bumpy career.

This is illustrated most forcefully in the final sequence of the film in which Jeannot returns to Marie's home as a man who seems to have lost his memories, and whose actions are now totally instinctive. The other main characters (Joëlle, Sanguine and Jean-François) scrutinise their friend, but seem not to recognise him either. In his absence, the relationships have been complicated a degree further (Sanguine goes into labour with Jean-François' baby). Marie's question, 'on est censé se dire quelque chose?' ('are we supposed to say something to each other?') can be understood on various levels: as an expression of confusion at the situation, of some bitterness at the reappearance of her former lover, but it is also a recognition of her role as an archetype, as a player in the unfolding drama of this film and of Blier's wider *œuvre*. Her assigning of roles earlier in the film ('si moi je suis la pro, alors tu dois être le maque': 'if I'm the prostitute, then you must be the pimp') is here interrogated: if they are no longer the same people as before (which they clearly are not), then who are they, and how should they behave? Behaviour is thus acknowledged as pure performance, and Blier's characters here recognise themselves for the pluralistic creations that they inevitably are, the sum of all their previous personae. Jeannot's response to this final question of Blier's filmic career to date provides us with the most profoundly intertextual moment in the entire corpus: 'Pardon', he says, 'pardon Marie, pardon les femmes.' ('Forgive me. Forgive me Marie, forgive me women.') The apology, the desire for reconciliation is expressed by a male character who has participated from both sides (provider and recipient) in the misogynistic discourse, the existence of which is not denied by the film; Jeannot's regretful articulation of his understanding of the nature of male–female relationships in the modern world, and his awareness that he is to be found wanting in this domain is an unusually intense conclusion for a Blier film. Blier's response to his own work, and to the accusations that have dogged his career is thus formulated beyond the scope of a formal interview, but in performance, where Blier expresses himself best of all.

Blier's distinctive cinematic vision of the modern urban experience would appear to have been concluded – at least for now – by the work of the trilogy. At a relatively late stage in his career Blier has now apparently left the cinema behind, and applied himself to writing for the theatre, and his first play, *Les Côtelettes*, starring Michel Bouquet and Philippe Noiret was staged at the Théâtre de la Porte-Saint-Martin in Paris in 1997. It is unclear whether or not this is a definitive career move, but Blier's admission that 'Plus j'avance dans la vie, plus je suis persuadé qu'un jour j'arrêterai de tourner pour ne plus faire qu'écrire' ('the older I get, the more convinced I become that one day I'll stop filming and only write'

(Garcin: 1997)) would appear to suggest that this return to his early career as a screen writer and novelist has so far proved to be both personally and creatively rewarding.

Interestingly, Blier's explanation for this movement towards the theatre resonates with disappointment, and appears to be, for him, a function of the consistent failure of the public and critics to understand his purpose. He claims to be lucid rather than bitter about this situation, declaring that 'Je vois bien que je ne suis plus en phase avec le public, que je suis trop âpre, rugueux, angoissé pour lui' ('I know that I'm out of step with the public, that I'm perceived as too harsh, too rough, too screwed up' (Garcin: 1997)). His remarks about the play (that 'Je destine ce texte à des spectateurs intelligents. Tout le contraire du public manipulé, conformiste, analphabète, parfois aveugle, sur lequel prospère désormais un cinéma jeuniste et abrutissant' (Garcin 1997: 54))[3] appear to suggest that what Blier feels he has failed to achieve, to his own personal satisfaction, is the complicit engagement of the film-viewing public upon which all authentic popular performance depends. Indeed, his disillusionment with modern cinema as an effective mode of artistic communication is here laid unambiguously at the feet of the passive, consumerist spectator. It is clear from these remarks that Blier's perception of his own success evidently lies not in commercial popularity *per se*, but rather in the successful fostering of the artist–spectator relationship, and his late exploration of the theatre as a mode of expression more suited to his perception of the importance of this relationship signals a renewed attempt to further impose his own particular concept of the popular in contemporary French popular performance. His admission that 'La mise-en-scène de cinéma a tendance à rendre imbécile. J'étais devenu un vieux réalisateur idiot et, aujourd'hui, grâce au théâtre, je me sens comme un jeune auteur' ('Film-making makes you crazy. I'd become a foolish old director, and now the theatre has made me feel like a young writer again' (Spira 1997: 4)) ultimately gives cause for real optimism as to the future creativity of this key French director.

3 'This play is aimed at intelligent spectators. The very opposite of the manipulated, conservative, illiterate often blind public which has allowed an immature, mindless cinema to thrive.'

References

Austin, Guy (1996) *Contemporary French Cinema*, Manchester, Manchester University Press.

Garcin, Jérôme (1997) 'Un deux trois théâtre', *Le Nouvel Observateur* 1713, 4 September.

Haustrate, Gaston (1988) *Bertrand Blier*, Paris, Edilig.

Pagnon, Gérard (1991) 'Merci la vie', *Télérama* 2148, 13 March, 26–7.

Spira, Alain (1997) 'Bertrand Blier envoie valser le cinéma pour le théâtre', *Paris Match*, 18 September, 3–5.

Toubiana, Serge (1991), 'Entretien avec Bertrand Blier', *Cahiers du cinéma* 441, 21–7.

Vecchi, Philippe (1993) 'J'aime les places où il n'y a pas un arbre', *Libération*, 18 August, 25–6.

Conclusion

Bertrand Blier's work is distinctive, innovative and highly original in modern French cinema, and both the mixed critical reception and variable commercial success that have greeted his work over a thirty-year period are evidence of his willingness, and indeed his ability to take risks with the cultural norms of mainstream film-making. As this book hopes to have shown, Blier's importance as a contemporary film-maker lies in three interrelated aspects of his work: first, in the way in which it accords with the French tradition of oppositional comment, and the source of this *contestataire* voice in cultures of marginality; second, in its evident investigation of the techniques of subversion fundamental to popular expression, particularly as they relate to narrative and dramatic construction; and finally in its exploration of a specifically dramatic intertext, particularly with respect to the traditional popular carnivalesque forms, which found renewed expression in modern French theatre practice in such movements as *café-théâtre*, absurd theatre and *création collective*.

The oppositional cultural context within which Blier's work can be located is one in which marginality is both the subject of investigation, and the ideological position from which the artistic motivation stems. Blier's relentless depiction of marginal charac-ters, their lifestyles and their position on the social and moral fringes of his diegetic societies is a key feature of his overall cine-matic conception, and one which has earned him the reputation of a misanthropist. However, Blier's consistent attention to the more

banal elements of social exchange reveals a considered devaluation of the accepted material of cinematic culture, together with an
explicit rejection of its norms and conventions, and demonstrates
a commitment to formulating, in form as well as content,
alternative processes of filmic narration. Blier's most significant
achievement is to have translated this rejection of the conventions
of established modes of cultural expression into an overarching
embrace of traditionally devalued low cultural forms, wherein
rejection for rejection's sake is not the primary motivation, but the
means by which 'low culture' can be made visible and valuable in
the cultural discourse.

Blier's contemporary characters are stock creations drawn from
long traditions of iconography and performance, and their construction as types, as amalgams of immediately familiar models,
affords a great sense of unreality to their actions, which in turn
serves as a forceful dramatic mechanism for conveying their
inability to integrate successfully into the modern urban world.
Contemporary life is perceived as 'too complicated' for the male
characters of *Les Valseuses*, *Préparez vos mouchoirs*, *Buffet froid* and
Tenue de soirée, a dilemma that the viewer is invited to empathise
with through the medium of comedy, expressed through the easy
camaraderie of the principal character relationships. Similarly, the
female protagonists of *Trop belle pour toi*, *Merci la vie*, *Un deux trois
soleil* and *Mon homme* express a desire to inhabit other temporal
dimensions, a condition that the viewer is invited to experience
through moments of narrative disjunction and expressions of
atemporal tranquillity, most commonly expressed through digressive monologue. These moments – comic and digressive – serve
to foster in Blier's films, against the depiction of unusual and at
times menacing environments and situations, an atmosphere of
absurdist familiarity, wherein the rules of logic and social interaction are patently otherwise. Thus, Blier's films are unusual in
the way in which they allow for the creation of a space where what
is not conventionally valued as cultural experience is recuperated
and made central to the expression.

Blier's work can be further contextualised in terms of wider
trends in French cultural discourse which, in the late 1960s and

early 1970s, witnessed a lessening of the 'thoroughly politicised and ideological perceptions of social and cultural life' and was followed instead by a 'general abandonment of an acute political consciousness' in the work of popular culture theorists and 'a general trend among French intellectuals from the early 1970s onwards to reject the atmosphere of politicisation, populism and revolutionary fantasy that characterised the years leading up to 1968' (Rigby 1991: 129–30). Blier's characters represent this trend: they are apolitical, self-interested and determinedly non-intellectual, the very antithesis of their immediate *nouvelle vague* forebears. Politics and revolution are not posited as potential solutions for these characters, but rather the thematic and dramatic focus of the films remains firmly on the minutiae of their modern urban existence. This concentration on the banal experiences of everyday life, free of attempts at aesthetic sanitisation, responds to the principles of ideological rejection outlined above, and is consistent with the more general trend in French cultural discourse identified by Kristin Ross where so much of the intellectual effort of the period – the earliest (and thus most materialist) works by Barthes and Baudrillard, for example, or that of the Situationists, Cornelius Castoriadis, Edgar Morin or Maurice Blanchot in his review essays of Lefèbvre – took the form of a theoretical reflection on 'everyday life' (Ross 1996: 5).

Blier's films seek to recreate an ancient or traditional concept of the popular, by innovatively reconsidering traditional forms with respect to non-linearity of narrative, permeable characterisation, temporal flexibility, modes of corporeality, and expressions of scatological humour. Blier presents these elements of his filmic construction as expressive of a specifically modern urban popular culture – fast-moving and at times chaotic action, unpredictable anti-heroes, hedonistic values, lack of coherence in crucial social relationships – yet the forms are intrinsically and importantly non-modern, and in fact perform the same function as the rituals of old folk culture, facilitating accessibility to a non-hegemonic cultural expression for a viewing public of varying degrees of artistic and educational sophistication. The distance that Blier thus takes in his work from former aesthetic modes in modern

French cinema, coupled with his embracing of forms entirely expressive of a post-new wave cinematic contemporaneity, is highly original in the field of modern French cinema.

Blier's cinema is a cinema which, in drawing on the traditions of popular dramatic cultures, is innovative in its rewriting of some of the rules of modern cinema. As we have seen through our analysis of Blier's films, an examination of the dominant performance styles of the genre of comedy that he promotes in modern cinema reveals that, far from leaving the theatre behind, one of the undercurrents of new wave polemic, this type of comedy in fact draws even more closely and more profitably on it; far from witnessing a definitive rupture between the traditions of theatre and film, a convergence established over the century in French cinema, modern comic film-making in fact sees a renewal of a process of particularly creative and commercially successful aesthetic transference. It is fair to say that the emergence of the *café-théâtre* into the cinema of the 1970s and 1980s very crucially revitalised, but also, and more importantly, transformed the long-standing relationship between theatre and popular cinema. With Blier's appropriation of the dramatic forms of the *café-théâtre*, and his promotion of them in mainstream film, this new creativity takes a clear direction in French cinema, acknowledging forms of theatre that are intrinsically dramatic, and themselves take a distance from notions of theatre as relayed by cinema in the twentieth century.

The subversive ethos of all authentically popular cultural expression is the second defining feature of Blier's approach to film-making, further emphasising his artistic and ideological marginality, and his consistency with wider French positions in cultural discourse and practice. Blier's cinema actively subverts traditional generic codes of narrative and performance, and the processes of subversion that he explores inform content, dramatic form and narrative construction in the films. His dramatic conception is original in its attention to structural forms which depend on circularity, subversion of physical and psychological consistency of character, narrative incoherence, and manipulation of register, and the films are striking in their intention to be nonreconciliatory in content and form. The concerted and consistent attack on authority, social convention, contemporary lifestyles, and social and intellectual pretension promoted in Blier's brand of comedy, strikes derisively at the heart of the cultural and social norms of French society, while his dramatic approach ironically attacks specifically French conventions of dramatic and cinematic expression. His attention to the depiction of socially subversive situations, the more or less uniform absence of a quality of reassurance or reassertion of the moral order in the narrative developments, and the overarching concept of ironic anti-illusionism that we find in his films all combine to set the *café-cinéma* genre of comedy, which Blier pioneers, outside the parameters of classical narrative comedy, and points to a deliberate abandonment and questioning of the conventions of social interaction. Furthermore, by drawing upon dominant practice in the domain of modern *théâtre populaire*, Blier's work forcefully challenges ideological assumptions about the nature and role of drama, its content and its performance.

Blier's investigation of Bakhtinian approaches to narrative construction wherein 'carnival is more than a mere festivity; it is the oppositional culture of the oppressed, the symbolic, anticipatory overthrow of oppressive social structures' (Stam 1992: 173) underlies his attention to processes of subversion, and allows him to mount a social, artistic and aesthetic challenge to the narrative and dramatic norms of mainstream cinema. His examination of utopian models of community, and his foregrounding of transgressive modes of being and behaviour, are echoed in the increased tendency in his later films towards spectacularisation, which in turn responds to the denunciation of the *'société de spectacle'* ('the society of the spectacle') led by Guy Debord and the Situationists, that is to say, the reaction against the relegation of the viewing public to the passive condition of spectators.[1] The

---

1 The situationists' denunciation of spectatorial passivity and constraint on creativity accords with Lefèbvre's critique of mass culture in *La Vie quotidienne dans le monde moderne* (Gallimard, 1968). See Rigby's discussion of this in Rigby (1991: 35–6). See also Guy Debord, *La Société du spectacle* (Buchet-Chastel, 1967), and Forbes (2000).

tensions which have long been apparent in evaluations of Blier's work are unsurprising when read in this context, where, as Stam argues, it is precisely the failure to acknowledge the carnival as a key source in modern popular culture that has resulted in the attitude of condescension that prevails with regard to certain film-makers: 'A number of film-makers[2] ... have been misunderstood or misappreciated because their work has been judged by the canons of "good taste" or "political correctness" rather than as prolongations of a perennial carnivalesque tradition. Carnival, for Bakhtin, is a valuable popular cultural source, "a proleptic of the avant-garde arts of expressionism and surrealism"' (Stam 1992: 98–9), which provides a valuable conceptual space for analysing discourses of marginality. Blier's major achievement as a contemporary film-maker has been to blur, successfully and, in keeping with the popular tradition controversially, the boundaries of cultural perception by introducing elements of the popular, the festive and what Bourdieu terms the 'barbaric' (Bourdieu 1984: 28–44), into the formally aesthetic domain of mainstream cultural production.

It is especially interesting that dramatic innovation and consequently cinematic dynamism of this kind should manifest itself in the context of the comic film, a genre which has tended to be perceived in film studies as the site of cultural decline rather than of cultural affirmation. Despite the critical contempt of the early years, the enduring success of Blier's films gives cause for optimism for the future of popular French national cinema. The close focus on traditional dramatic forms drawn directly from French popular culture can arguably be read as a positive and forceful affirmation of cultural specificity in the face of an ever-threatening post-GATT global film culture.

2 Stam (1992: 115). Stam's specific reference is to the work of the directors Federico Fellini and Pier Paulo Pasolini.

References

Bourdieu, Pierre (1984) *Distinction: a Critique of the Social Judgement of Taste* (trans. Richard Nice), London, Routledge.

Debord, Guy (1967) *La Société du Spectacle*, Paris, Buchet-Chastel.

Forbes, Jill (2000) 'Sex, Politics and Popular Culture: Bertrand Blier's *Les Valseuses* (1973)' in Susan Hayward and Ginette Vincendeau, *French Film: Texts and Contexts*, 2nd edn, London and New York, Routledge, 213–26.

Lefèbvre, Henri (1968) *La Vie quotidienne dans le monde moderne*, Paris, Gallimard.

Rigby, Brian (1991) *Popular Culture in Modern France: a Study of Cultural Discourse*, London and New York, Routledge.

Ross, Kristin (1996) *Fast Cars, Clean Bodies: Decolonization and the Reordering of French Culture*, Cambridge, MA, MIT Press.

Stam, Robert (1992) *Subversive Pleasures: Bakhtin, Cultural Criticism and Film*, Baltimore, Johns Hopkins University Press.

Filmography

Hitler, connais pas! (1963) 100 min.

Screenplay: Bertrand Blier
Direction: Bertrand Blier
Photography (b&w): Jean-Louis Picavet
Editing: Michèle Davis
Sound: Robert Biart
Music: Georges Delerue
Cast: Non-professional cast.
Production: André Michelin/Chaumiane

Presented for the Semaine de la Critique, Cannes 1963; 'Voile d'Argent' at the Locarno Film Festival, July 1963

La Grimace (1966) (court métrage)

No production details available

Même si j'étais un espion (1967) 95 min.

Screenplay: Antoine Tudal, Jean-Pierre Simonot, Jacques Cousseau, Philippe Adrien, Bertrand Blier
Direction: Bertrand Blier
Photography (b&w): Jean-Louis Picavet
Editing: Kenout Peltier
Sound: Guy Rophé
Artistic direction: Marc Désages
Music: Serge Gainsbourg
Cast: Bernard Blier (Dr Lefèvre), Bruno Cremer (Matras), Suzanne Flon (Geneviève Laurent), Patricia Scot (Sylvie Lefèvre), Claude Piéplu (Monteil)
Production: Pathé/Sirius/UGC/CFDC

Les Valseuses (1973) 117 min.

Screenplay: Bertrand Blier, Philippe Dumarcay (from the novel by Bertand Blier)
Direction: Bertrand Blier
Photography: Bruno Nuytten
Editing: Kenout Peltier
Sound: Dominique Dalmasso
Artistic direction: Jean-Jacques Caziot
Music: Stéphane Grappelli
Cast: Gérard Depardieu (Jean-Claude), Patrick Dewaere (Pierrot), Miou-Miou (Marie-Ange), Jeanne Moreau (Jeanne), Jacques Chailleux (Jacques), Brigitte Fossey (breast-feeding mother), Isabelle Huppert (Jacqueline), Gérard Jugnot
Production: CAPAC/Uranus/UPF/Prodis

Calmos (1976) 107 min.

Screenplay: Bertrand Blier, Philippe Dumarcay
Direction: Bertrand Blier
Photography: Claude Renoir
Editing: Claudine Merlin
Sound: William Sivel
Artistic direction: Jean André
Music: Georges Delerue
Cast: Jean-Pierre Marielle (Paul Dufour), Jean Rochefort (Albert), Bernard Blier (priest), Brigitte Fossey (Suzanne Dufour), Claude Piéplu (old soldier), Micheline Kahn (Geneviève), Dora Doll (sergeant), Nicole Garcia, Valérie Mairesse
Production: Christian Fechner/Renn Productions

Préparez vos mouchoirs (1978) 108 min.

Screenplay: Bertrand Blier
Direction: Bertrand Blier
Photography: Jean Penzer
Editing: Claudine Merlin
Sound: Jean-Pierre Ruh
Artistic direction: Eric Moulard
Music: Georges Delerue, Mozart, Schubert
Cast: Gérard Depardieu (Raoul), Patrick Dewaere (Stéphane), Carole Laure (Solange), Riton (Christian Belœil), Michel Serrault (neighbour), Eléonore Hirt (Mme Belœil), Sylvie Joly (passer-by), Jean Rougerie (M. Belœil)
Production: Films Ariane/CAPAC/Belga Films/SODEP

Academy Award for Best Foreign Film 1979

Buffet froid (1979) 95 min.

Screenplay: Bertrand Blier
Direction: Bertrand Blier

Photography: Jean Penzer
Editing: Claudine Merlin
Sound: Jean-Pierre Ruh
Artistic direction: Théo Meurisse
Music: Brahms
Cast: Gérard Depardieu (Alphonse Tram), Bernard Blier (l'inspecteur Morvan-
    dieu), Jean Carmet (murderer), Geneviève Page (widow), Michel Serrault
    (le quidam), Jean Rougerie (witness), Carole Bouquet (quidam's daughter).
Production: Sara Films/Antenne 2

César for Best Original Screenplay, 1980

Beau-père (1981) 120 min.

Screenplay: Bertrand Blier (from the novel by Bertrand Blier)
Direction: Bertrand Blier
Photography: Sacha Vierny
Editing: Claudine Merlin
Artistic direction: Théo Meurisse
Music: Philippe Sarde, Bach
Cast: Patrick Dewaere (Rémi), Ariel Besse (Marion), Maurice Ronet (Charly),
    Nicole Garcia (Martine), Nathalie Baye (Charlotte)
Production: Sara Films/Antenne 2

Sélection officielle, Cannes 1981

La Femme de mon pote (1983) (My Best Friend's Girl) 99 min.

Screenplay: Bertrand Blier, Gérard Brach
Direction: Bertrand Blier
Photography: Jean Penzer
Editing: Claudine Merlin
Sound: Bernard Bats
Artistic direction: Théo Meurisse
Music: J. J. Cale, Mozart
Cast: Coluche (Mickey), Isabelle Huppert (Viviane), Thierry Lhermitte (Pascal),
    François Perrot (Doctor)
Production: Alain Sarde for Sara Films/Renn Productions

Notre histoire (1984) 110 min.

Screenplay: Bertrand Blier
Direction: Bertrand Blier
Photography: Jean Penzer
Editing: Claudine Merlin
Sound: Bernard Bats, Dominique Hennequin
Artistic direction: Bernrad Evein
Music: Laurent Rossi, Beethoven, Schubert, Bohuslav Martinu

Cast: Alain Delon (Robert Avranche), Nathalie Baye (Donatienne Pouget/
Marie-Thérèse Chatelard/Geneviève Avranche), Michel Galabru (Emile),
Gérard Darmon (Duval), Sabine Haudepin (Carmen)
Production: Alain Sarde for Sara Films/Adel Productions

Césars for Best Actor (Alain Delon), Best Original Screenplay, 1984

Tenue de soirée (1986) 84 min.

Screenplay: Bertrand Blier
Direction: Bertrand Blier
Photography: Jean Penzer
Editing: Claudine Merlin
Sound: Bernard Bats, Dominique Hennequin
Artistic Direction: Théo Meurisse
Music: Serge Gainsbourg
Cast: Gérard Depardieu (Bob), Michel Blanc (Antoine), Miou-Miou (Monique),
Bruno Cremer (Art collector), Jean-Pierre Marielle (L'homme dépressif),
Michel Creton (Pedro)
Production: René Cleitman for Hachette Première/Philippe Dussart
Productions/Ciné Valse/DD Productions

César for Best Actor (Michel Blanc), 1986.

Trop belle pour toi (1989) 91 min.

Screenplay: Bertrand Blier
Direction: Bertrand Blier
Photography: Philippe Rousselot
Editing: Claudine Merlin
Sound: Stéphane Granel
Artistic direction: Théo Meurisse
Music: Schubert
Cast: Gérard Depardieu (Bernard Barthélemy), Josiane Balasko (Colette
Chevasus), Carole Bouquet (Florence Barthélemy), François Cluzet (Pascal),
Roland Blanche (Marcello), Miriam Boyer (Geneviève)
Production: Bernard Marescot for Ciné Valse/DD Productions/Orly Films/
Sedif/TF1 Films

Prix spécial du jury, Cannes 1989; Césars for Best Film, Best Director (Bertrand
Blier), Best Actress (Carole Bouquet), Best Original Screenplay, Best
Editing (Claudine Merlin), all 1990; Prix de l'Académie des Arts et
Techniques du Cinéma 1990

Merci la vie (1991) 113 min.

Screenplay: Bertrand Blier
Direction: Bertrand Blier
Photography: Philippe Rousselot

Editing: Claudine Merlin
Sound: Pierre Gamet
Artistic Direction: Théo Meurisse
Music: Philippe Glass, Jacques Brel, David Byrne, Beethoven, Chopin, Puccini, Vivaldi
Cast: Charlotte Gainsbourg (Camille Pelleveau), Anouk Grinberg (Joëlle), Gérard Depardieu (Marc-Antoine), Michel Blanc (Raymond Pelleveau, young), Jean Carmet (Raymond Pelleveau, old), Jean-Louis Trintignant (German officer), Annie Girardot (Camille's mother, old), Catherine Jacob (Camille's mother, young), Jean Rougerie (doctor)
Production: Bernard Marescot for Ciné Valse/Film par Film/Orly Films/DD Productions/Sedif/Films A2

César for Best Supporting Actor (Jean Carmet), 1992

Un deux trois soleil (1994) 104 min.
Screenplay: Bertrand Blier
Direction: Bertrand Blier
Photography: Gérard de Battista
Editing: Claudine Merlin
Sound: Pierre Belve, Paul Bertault
Artistic direction: Théo Meurisse, Jean-Jacques Caziot, Georges Glon
Music: Khaled, Anton Bruckner, Gabriel Fauré
Cast: Anouk Grinberg (Victorine), Myriam Boyer (Victorine's mother), Marcello Mastroianni (Victorine's father), Irène Tassembedo (Gladys), Olivier Martinez (Petit Paul), Jean-Michel Noirey, Denise Chalem, Jean-Pierre Marielle, Claude Brasseur
Production: Gaumont/Ciné Valse/France 3 Cinéma

Mon homme (1996) (My Man) 98 min.
Screenplay: Bertrand Blier
Direction: Bertrand Blier
Photography: Pierre Lhomme
Editing: Claudine Merlin
Sound: Pierre Gamet
Artistic direction: Willy Holt, Georges Glon
Music: Barry White, Henryk Mikolaj Gorecki
Cast: Anouk Grinberg (Marie Arbath), Gérard Lanvin (Jeannot), Valéria Bruni-Tedeschi (Sanguine), Olivier Martinez (Jean-François), Sabine Azéma (Bérangère), Michel Galabru (client), Jean-Pierre Léaud (M. Claude), Mathieu Kassovitz (client)
Production: Alain Sarde/Plateau A with Studio Images 2 and the participation of Canal+

Select bibliography

See also the References sections at the end of each chapter

Books, book chapters and journal articles on Blier's films

Austin, Guy 'History and Spectacle in Blier's *Merci la vie*', *French Cultural Studies* 5, 1994, 73–84. A perceptive analysis of *Merci la vie* in relation to questions of spectatorship, testimony and the representation of history. Austin's discussion of the tension between voyeuristic pleasure and disturbing historical spectacle is particularly revealing.

Austin, Guy *Contemporary French Cinema*, Manchester, Manchester University Press, 1996. Blier's work is discussed as part of an overview of French cinema in the 1980s and 1990s. *Les Valseuses, Tenue de soirée* and *Merci la vie* are read in terms of the challenge they present to established cinematic genres, in particular in their treatment of the representation of sexuality.

Forbes, Jill 'In Search of the Popular Cinema: New French Comedy' in *The Cinema in France: After the New Wave*, London, Macmillan, 1992, 171–88. Forbes's chapter was the first sustained study of Blier's work in English. Her analysis of the comic mechanisms at work in Blier's films up to *Trop belle pour toi* (1989), and her very full discussion of Blier's exploration of masculinity and questions of sexual identity have paved the way for other scholars, myself included, to assess Blier's contribution to modern French film-making. Her book provides essential information about the post-1968 context in which Blier's films emerged, and the chapter highlights the significance of the *café-théâtre* to both his work and working methods.

Forbes, Jill 'Sex, Politics and Popular Culture: Bertrand Blier's *Les Valseuses* (1973)' in Susan Hayward and Ginette Vincendeau, *French Film: Texts and Contexts*, 2nd edn, London and New York, Routledge, 2000, 213–26. This recent essay re-evaluates *Les Valseuses* almost thirty years after its release, and points to its importance both as a social document and as a ground-breaking example of post-new wave cinema. The discussion of Godardian intertextuality in this film is especially illuminating.

Harris, Sue 'The People's Filmmaker? Popular Theatre and the Films of Bertrand Blier' in Sheila Perry and Marie Cross (eds), *Voices of France: Social, Political and Cultural Identity*, London and Washington, Pinter, 1997, 114–26. This essay examines Blier's work in terms of traditions of popular performance, and their influence on French theatre practice in the 1960s and 1970s. It argues the case that the popular dimension of Blier's work is stylistically consistent with a specifically theatrical concept.

Harris, Sue '*Hitler, connais pas!* Bertrand Blier's Apprenticeship in the Techniques of Spectacle', *French Cultural Studies* (special edition on 100 years of French cinema, edited by Keith Reader) 7 (1996), 295–307. This essay provides a detailed analysis of Blier's first film, and invites a reading of it as a formative work in his *œuvre*. Although apparently very different in methodology and content from the commercially successful fiction films of Blier's mature career, the film is presented as one which, in fact, laid the ground for the innovations in style and form that we have come to associate with Blier.

Harris, Sue '*Les comiques font de la résistance*: Dramatic Trends in Popular Film Comedy', *Australian Journal of French Studies* (special edition on popular culture in post-war France), March 1998, 86–99. This essay examines the impact of the *café-théâtre* on modern film comedy, using the work of Blier and the Splendid theatre group as examples.

Harris, Sue, and King, Russell S. *Bertrand Blier and Misogyny*, Stirling French Publications, 4, 1996. This short work includes responses by each of the authors to the accusation of misogyny levelled at Blier by critics and scholars throughout his career. King's essay, 'Bertrand Blier's Men Behaving Badly: the Question of Misogyny' (1–11) argues that postmodern insecurity about masculinity and male identity is translated in Blier's work into a generalised social misanthropy, which has been misinterpreted by critics as misogyny. The second essay, 'Image, Position, Performance: Misogyny and the Female Subject in the Films of Bertrand Blier' (12–23) argues for a recognition of the complexity and originality of female roles and performances in Blier's work, which have so far remained obscured by facile and superficial readings of the director's 'misogyny'.

Haustrate, Gaston *Bertrand Blier*, Paris, Edilig, 1988. This well-sustained study of Blier's early work from *Hitler, connais pas!* (1963) to *Tenue de Soirée* (1986) combines interviews with Blier with thematic and stylistic analysis of individual films. At the time of publication, this remains the only book in French on the director's work.

Mesnil, Michel, '*Merci la vie* ou l'imaginaire à la française', *Esprit*, May 1991, 126–35. Mesnil offers a persuasive reading of *Merci la vie* as a film about the imagination, in this case that of an adolescent girl revising for her *baccalauréat*. The main body of the film is explained by the author as a projection of nightmarish and often subversive fantasies, conflating history (the subject being revised) and sexual experiences (whether real or imagined).

Powrie, Phil, *'Tenue de soirée*: the "Suffering Macho"' in *French Cinema in the 1980s: Nostalgia and the Crisis of Masculinity*, Oxford, Clarendon Press, 1997, 171–82. Powrie uses the example of Depardieu in *Tenue de soirée* to conclude his discussion of the crisis in masculinity in modern French culture as mediated by contemporary film-makers. Powrie examines the challenge to received notions of masculinity represented by Depardieu/Bob in the film, and argues that the actor/character is a problematic, but emblematic figure, in what he identifies as the repositioning of masculinity in 1980s cinema.

Interviews with Blier and his principal actors

Alion, Yves 'Entretien avec Bertrand Blier', *Revue du cinéma* 417, June 1986, 49–50.

Alion, Yves 'Entretien avec Miou-Miou: des *Valseuses* à *Tenue de soirée*', *Revue du cinéma* 417, June 1986, 57–8.

Audé, Françoise and Jeancolas, Jean-Pierre 'Entretien avec Bertrand Blier', *Positif*, May 1989, 6–11.

Chevrie, Marc and Dubroux, Danièle 'A la recherche de l'histoire: entretien avec Bertrand Blier', *Cahiers du cinéma* 371/2, May 1985, 12–13.

Cuel, François and Carcassonne, Philippe 'Entretien avec Bernard Blier', *Cinématographe* 54, January 1980, 40–4.

Cuel, François and Carcassonne, Philippe 'Entretien avec Bertrand Blier' *Cinématographe* 54, January 1980, 45–8.

Dufreigne, Jean-Pierre 'Je tourne par mauvaise humeur', *L'Express*, 19 August 1993, 52.

Douin, Jean-Luc 'Entretien avec Miou-Miou', *Télérama* 1359, 28 January 1976, 60–1.

Garcin, Jérôme 'Un deux trois théâtre', *Le Nouvel Observateur* 1713, 4 September 1997, 54.

Halberstadt, Michèle and Moriconi, Martine 'Le perturbateur tranquille: entretien avec Bertrand Blier', *Première* 109, April 1986, 78–9 and 171–4.

Jousse, Thierry 'Rencontre avec Josiane Balasko', *Cahiers du cinéma* 489, March 1995, 62–3.

Lavoignat, Jean-Pierre 'Entretien avec Miou-Miou', *Première* 109, April 1986, 81 and 176.

'Le Bon Plaisir de Bertrand Blier', broadcast by France Culture, 18 February 1995.

Le Guay, Philippe 'Entretien avec Bertrand Blier', *Cinématographe* 119, May 1986, 20–3.

Maillet, Dominique 'Entretien avec Miou-Miou', *Cinématographe* 24, February 1977, 22–3.

Martin, Marcel '*Hitler, connais pas!* Onze jeunes devant la caméra-question de Bertrand Blier', *Les Lettres françaises*, 2 May 1963, 1 and 6.

Michaux, Sylvie 'Bertrand Blier: Une fantastique admiration pour la femme...' *Le Nouvel Observateur* 1119, 18 April 1986, 60.

Pagnon, Gérard 'Entretien avec Bertrand Blier: Un film, c'est un hold-up', *Télérama* 2148, 13 March 1991, 24–6.

Spira, Alain 'Bertrand Blier envoie valser le cinéma pour le théâtre', *Paris Match*, 18 September 1997, 3–5.

Toubiana, Serge 'Les mots et les choses: entretien avec Bertrand Blier' *Cahiers du cinéma* 382, April 1986, 9–65.

Toubiana, Serge 'La baguette magique: entretien avec Michel Blanc', *Cahiers du cinéma* 382, April 1986, 11–12.

Toubiana, Serge 'Josiane Balasko, Bertrand Blier: jeux de mots, jeux d'acteurs', *Cahiers du cinéma* 407–8, May 1988, 12–17.

Toubiana, Serge and Jousse, Thierry 'Entretien avec Bertrand Blier: la truculence, le fantastique et le sentimental', *Cahiers du cinéma* 419/20, May 1989, 68–71.

Toubiana, Serge 'Entretien avec Bertrand Blier', *Cahiers du cinéma* 441, March 1991, 22–7.

Vecchi, Philippe 'J'aime les places où il n'y a pas un arbre', *Libération*, 18 August 1993, 25–6.

Works by Blier

Les Valseuses, Laffont (Paris, 1972).

Buffet froid, Avant-scène du Cinéma 244, 15 March 1980.

Beau-père, Laffont (Paris, 1981).

Les Côtelettes, Actes Sud (Paris, 1997).

Existe en blanc, Laffont (Paris, 1998)

Index